Gill & Macmillan
Annotated Constitution
of Ireland

Dedication of J. A. Foley

For my Mother, for Gráinne and for O.P.M.

Dedication of Stephen Lalor

GGmC
ALUE

Gill & Macmillan Annotated Constitution of Ireland 1937-1994

With Commentary

EDITORS

J. Anthony Foley *Barrister-at-Law*

and

Stephen Lalor *B.A.(Mod.), M.Litt., Ph.D.*

Gill & Macmillan

Gill & Macmillan Ltd
Goldenbridge
Dublin 8
with associated companies throughout the world

© Gill & Macmillan 1995

0 7171 2276 X

Index compiled by Julitta Clancy
Print origination by Typeform Repro Limited, Dublin
Printed by ColourBooks Limited, Dublin

A catalogue record is available for this book from the British Library.

Contents

Foreword

FOREWORD

In recent years we have seen the publication of a number of scholarly works on the Irish Constitution. This is a reflection of the immense impact which the Constitution has on our daily lives as citizens of Ireland. The Constitution is the pre-eminent legal document of this State and as such it is to be expected that numerous books would be written concerning various aspects of it.

It is appropriate to recall the beginning of the preface to the first edition of the *Law of Contract* by Cheshire and Fifoot where the authors in turn invoked the philosopher Paley who had remarked that 'when a writer offers a book to the public upon a subject on which the public are already in possession of many others, he is bound by a kind of literary justice to inform his readers, distinctly and specifically, what it is he professes to supply and what he expects to improve'.[1] In order for any new book to be worthwhile it must possess at least one of two qualities: it must deal with an entirely new subject matter; or adopt a new perspective on one already established.

I believe the authors of this book have succeeded on both counts. This book does not purport to compete with mainstream legal texts on the Constitution, nor does it attempt to queer the pitch, so to speak, of authors who have written on the political background to the drafting of the Constitution. The authors have filled a lacuna which existed in academic writing on the Constitution. They have, with diligence and accuracy, traced the development of the Constitution through its various amendments. Considerable reference is made, throughout this text, to Oireachtas reports, thus providing a flavour of the legislative arena from which the constitutional amendments emanated. There have been thirteen amendments made to the 1937 Constitution. The first two were made by the Oireachtas

---

1. Preface to the *Principles of Moral and Political Philosophy* by William Paley. [The publication was justified; it went to fifteen editions in the author's lifetime.]

during the transitory three year period after the first President took office, when it was unnecessary to hold a referendum. The third amendment was not effected until 1972 although during the thirty-one-year interval two failed attempts had been made to abolish proportional representation as the method of voting.

The publication of this book brings into focus the question of whether a Constitution is something which should be frequently amended or indeed periodically redrafted. It is claimed by some critics that a document written in the 1930s must fail to take account of modern realities and that we should have a new Constitution every now and again. But as Edmund Burke reminds us:

'A man full of warm speculative benevolence may wish his society otherwise constituted than he finds it; but a good patriot, and a true politician, always considers how he shall make the most of the existing materials of his country. A disposition to preserve, and an ability to improve, taken together would be my standard of a statesman. Everything else is vulgar in the conception, perilous in the execution.'[2]

It is also pertinent to point out that our Constitution contains a fundamental rights section that pre-dated by ten years the Universal Declaration on Human Rights proclaimed by the United Nations General Assembly in December 1948. It was a further two years before the European Convention on Human Rights and Fundamental Freedoms was signed at Rome.

It was the stated wish of the chief draftsman of the Constitution, Mr Eamon de Valera, that the Courts should construe the Constitution liberally. Mr de Valera was concerned lest the Courts would adopt a 'strictly legalistic' view of the Constitution, thereby limiting its scope.[3] Mr Sean Lemass, as Taoiseach, wished that the Supreme Court

2. *Reflections on the Revolution in France.*
3. *Dáil Éireann Debates,* Vol. 67, pp. 53-4; 427-8.

would adopt the activism of the Supreme Court of the United States of America as a model.[4] Their wish for a liberal interpretation of the Constitution has probably been realised beyond their expectations. The vibrancy of the Constitution has been demonstrated by the Supreme Court decisions in—to mention but a few—*Ryan v The Attorney General*,[5] *Byrne v Ireland*,[6] *Meskell v CIE*,[7] and *McGee v The Attorney General*.[8] The process of judicial review serves to ensure that this will continue to be the case.

This book will have very broad appeal. It is as relevant to the student of political science as it is to the student of modern Irish history. It also represents a most worthy addition to the numerous fine legal texts already published on the Constitution. I heartily congratulate the authors on their outstanding work and I commend this book not only to legal practitioners but also to the general public. I am sure all who read it will derive much enjoyment from it.

Hugh O'Flaherty

The Supreme Court
Four Courts
Dublin
2 May 1994

---

4. See the interview with Mr Justice Walsh in *Judging the World*, Butterworths, 1988 pp. 418-9.
5. [1965] IR 294.
6. [1972] IR 241.
7. [1973] IR 121.
8. [1974] IR 284.

Preface

PREFACE

This work is intended to be purely descriptive of *Bunreacht na hÉireann*, the so-called 1937 Constitution of Ireland, and has a two-fold objective. The first is that of producing a complete text of the Constitution which incorporates the changes it has undergone since its adoption by the people in 1937—a so called 'collated' text. The second is to provide background information in the form of brief annotated extracts from the Oireachtas debates to demonstrate just how these changes came about and to describe the process of amendment in each case. The extracts from the Oireachtas debates were chosen to be either representative or interesting. Sometimes a lone voice made a point not touched upon by other speakers but which seemed to be of interest. On other occasions brief reference was made to very diverse areas of interest and it seemed necessary to mention these subjects in passing only.

The book is arranged in chronological order. The note on the Report of the Commission on the Constitution is of particular interest because it was published at the mid-point between the enactment of the Constitution and the present day. It is possible, therefore to see the development of the Constitution over the period of its existence.

This unofficial text of the Constitution is a copy of the text published prior to the 1937 referendum and voted on by the people in 1937 together with the subsequent amendments passed by the Oireachtas and voted on in referendum. The Transitory Provisions, Articles 51 to 63 inclusive, which continue to have the force of law, are included in the unofficial text. In accordance with Articles 51 and 52 of the Constitution the official text is required to omit these Articles.

In this *Gill & Macmillan* edition, the text is laid out in a unique manner. The Constitution as passed in 1937 is printed in ordinary type. Articles and portions of Articles which have been deleted are printed with a line drawn through them ~~thus~~ and insertions are highlighted by a grey background. References to the appropriate amending Acts are given in numbered footnotes. Amendments have been incorporated into the text in such a way that it should be possible to recreate the text as it was at any particular time.

The Irish text is not given here primarily because it is not possible to produce a sufficiently authoritative text in the same form as the English text. The reader is referred to Richard Humphrey's *The Constitution of Ireland: The forgotten textual quagmire*[9] which brought to light, particularly in relation to the Irish text:

> 'The surprising degree of discordance which exists between the various texts of the Constitution, the draft debated in 1937, the subsequent editions of 1938, 1942 and 1980, the Amending Acts, and the text made available to the public by the Stationery Office.'

The reader should note that although there is an Eleventh Amendment Act and a Thirteenth Amendment Act, there is no Twelfth Amendment Act. The Twelfth Amendment of the Constitution Bill, 1992, voted on the same day as the Eleventh Amendment Act, 1992, and the Thirteenth Amendment Act, 1992, was rejected by the people.

Due to restrictions on space, we do not intend to give details of cases to which reference is made as to do so would be to introduce a mass of material not relevant to the argument.

The great pleasure in having a book published is to be able to thank those who have been of assistance during its gestation. We thank Mr Michael O'Donoghue, now Assistant Secretary in the Department of Defence for help with the text of early drafts of the Constitution and with Bills and Acts of the various Amendments of the Constitution. We

---

9. *The Irish Jurist* vol. XXII, (new series) part 2, Winter 1987, pp. 169-78.

thank Professor Robert Heuston for his encouragement at the beginning of the work, and with the text of the Constitution as published in 1942. We are particularly grateful to the Honourable Mr Justice Hugh O'Flaherty of the Supreme Court for his most valuable comments and suggestions and for his generous foreword to our work. We would also like to thank the following people: Professor William Binchy, Trinity College, for his advice and encouragement; Col. Patrick Ghent, BL, Deputy Judge Advocate General; Comdt Desmond Hogan, BL and Comdt Patrick Godfrey, BL of the Office of the Deputy Judge Advocate General; Ms Elizabeth Sheehan, Department of Equality and Law Reform; *The Irish Times* Library; Brendan Mahony, Military Archives, Cathal Brugha Barracks; and Mr Jonathan Armstrong, Librarian, The Honorable Society of King's Inns. Our thanks also go to Mr Robin Hannan for all the material he placed at our disposal and to Louisa Edwards for her Herculean efforts of proof reading.

J. Anthony Foley
Stephen Lalor
17 June 1994

TABLE OF CASES

TABLE OF AMENDMENTS TO THE CONSTITUTION

Title of Amendment	Date of coming into effect
First Amendment of the Constitution Act, 1939.	2 September 1939
Second Amendment of the Constitution Act, 1941.	30 May 1941
Third Amendment of the Constitution Act, 1972.	8 June 1972
Fourth Amendment of the Constitution Act, 1972 and Fifth Amendment of the Constitution Act, 1972.	5 January 1973
Sixth Amendment of the Constitution (Adoption) Act, 1979.	3 August 1979
Seventh Amendment of the Constitution (Election of Members of Seanad Éireann by Institutions of Higher Education) Act, 1979.	3 August 1979
Eighth Amendment of the Constitution Act, 1983.	7 October 1983
Ninth Amendment of the Constitution Act, 1984.	2 August 1984
Tenth Amendment of the Constitution Act, 1987.	22 June 1987
Eleventh Amendment of the Constitution Act, 1992.	16 July 1992
Thirteenth Amendment of the Constitution Act 1992 and Fourteenth Amendment of the Constitution Act, 1992.	23 December 1992

Introduction

INTRODUCTION

CONSTITUTIONAL CHANGE

One purpose of this work is to show how *Bunreacht na hÉireann* (The Constitution of Ireland) has been amended since the Irish people accepted it in 1937. It will also look briefly and discursively at some amendments of the Free State Constitution of 1922 which undermined the Free State Constitution itself. There is, in addition, the transition from the Constitution of the Irish Free State to the Constitution of Ireland, for, as we shall see, the introduction of the Constitution of Ireland was seen by some to be no more than the amendment of the Free State Constitution. As a prelude to that exercise it is useful to look briefly at the methods employed in different countries to bring about constitutional amendment.

When a Constitution is being adopted or amended provision is usually made for some form of consultation with the people. This is in keeping with the doctrine of the sovereignty of the people and acknowledges the fact that the people should adopt a Constitution and that it should be changed only with their consent given either directly by referendum or indirectly through an elected parliament.

How does one determine the wishes of the people in this context? Under the Irish Constitution of 1937, as under others such as those of Australia and Denmark, the proposed amendment is referred to the people by referendum, having first gone through the legislature. This method endows the people with direct and very real power when there is any question of amendment.

In some countries, the Constitution gives the legislature the power to make an amendment, with the proviso that this will be followed by a general election. The election result will show whether the people are willing or not to sanction the amendment. Belgium employs a derivative of this method, as do Norway, Sweden and the Netherlands.

A third method for achieving amendment is by reference to the people in certain specified circumstances. In France, for instance, a referendum need not take place if the amendment in question has been carried by a three-fifths majority of both Houses of Parliament at a joint sitting convened for that purpose.

A further approach to amendment is the initiative whereby the people may propose amendments. This procedure is provided for under the Swiss Constitution and under the Constitutions of some of the American States. Article 48 of the 1922 Constitution of Saorstát Éireann provided for the introduction of legislation which would permit the introduction of the initiative concept. Before the legislation was passed, however, these provisions were removed by the Constitution (Amendment No. 10) Act, 1928.

K. C. Wheare, in *Modern Constitutions*, considers that uniformity in the amending process is not entirely necessary and he suggests:

> 'It would be perfectly proper to say that some parts of a Constitution may be altered by a simple majority of the legislature, that other parts may be altered only with the approval of the people.'

He gives as an example the Indian Constitution, a federal constitution, which provides for two forms of amendment process. The fact that these relate to the federal nature of the Union may weaken Professor Wheare's point. He concedes that examples of variety in the amending process are rare.

Given that the Irish people adopted *Bunreacht na hÉireann* by plebiscite (and see also the words of the Preamble in this respect), it is unlikely that they would accept amendment by any method other than by referendum.

Under Article 46 any provision of the Constitution may be amended, including Article 46 itself. As provided in Article 46.2, any Bill to amend the Constitution must be initiated in Dáil Éireann and once it has passed both Houses of the Oireachtas, the Bill must be submitted to referendum by the people, whose decision is by a majority of the votes cast. Any such Bill must be expressed to be 'An Act to amend the Constitution' and may contain only the proposal, or proposals, to amend the Constitution. In all respects such a Bill follows the usual course of Bills through both Houses of the Oireachtas.

In accordance with Article 47.4, various Acts have been passed which 'regulated by law' the process of referendum in accordance with the Article.[10] It is worthwhile to contrast this with the previous Constitution.

THE CONSTITUTION OF 1922

The Constitution of 1922 consisted of the First Schedule to the Irish Free State (Saorstát Éireann) Act, 1922 (No. 1 of 1922). The Second Schedule of that Act comprised 'Articles of Agreement for a Treaty between Great Britain and Ireland'. Both Schedules were constitutionally significant.

In January 1922, Michael Collins,[11] President of the Provisional Government, established a Constitutional Committee, of which he was Chairman, to address the matter of drafting a constitution. Collins and Lloyd George

---

10. Referendum Act, 1942 (No. 8 of 1942).
    Electoral Act, 1963 (No. 19 of 1963).
    Electoral (Amendment) Act, 1972 (No. 4 of 1972).
    Electoral (Amendment) Act, 1973 (No. 3 of 1973).
    Electoral (Amendment) Act, 1986 (No. 12 of 1986).
    Electoral Act, 1992 (No. 23 of 1992).
11. General Michael Collins (1890-1922): Joined Irish Republican Brotherhood in 1915; served as Aide-de-Camp to Count Plunkett during the 1916 Insurrection and was subsequently interned in Frangoch; Adjutant General, Irish Volunteers and controlled the intelligence function during the War of Independence; elected to the First Dáil in 1919; served as Minister of Home Affairs and subsequently as Minister for Finance, becoming President of the Provisional Government. Collins reluctantly became head of the delegation sent to London to negotiate the Treaty. At the outbreak of the civil war he became Commander-in-Chief of the Free State Army and was killed in action on 20 August 1922.

had agreed, prior to this, that the Draft Constitution would be shown to the British cabinet for approval before its publication by the Provisional Government. By this time the pro- and anti-Treaty factions were on the point of civil war. To avert this Eamon de Valera[12] and Collins reached an understanding to the effect that if a Constitution which basically reflected the sovereignty of the Irish people without reference to the Treaty or to the British connection could be drafted, de Valera would be willing to cooperate.

Collins appointed the Committee. Darrell Figgis was Vice-Chairman and members included people active in the Irish White Cross, barristers, university professors and others. Collins required expertise in constitutional matters but in the interest of impartiality tried to appoint people who were above politics.[13] Nevertheless, the document which this Committee produced, despite its merits in the normal constitutional sense, was enshrined in the Treaty which became the springboard for the Irish Civil War.

This deprived the Constitution of one of the essential attributes of effective constitutions, namely, its role as the instrument of supreme law. Article 2 of the 1922 Constitution stated that:

> 'all powers of government and all authority, legislative, executive and judicial are derived from the People of Ireland . . . '

But section 2 of the Constitution of the Irish Free State (Saorstát Éireann) Act, 1922 provided that:

---

12. Eamon de Valera: Born in New York in 1882; 'returned' to Ireland at the age of three; condemned to death in 1916 but reprieved. President of the Irish Volunteers, 1917–26; President of the Executive Council, 1932-7; Taoiseach, 1937-48 and on a number of later occasions. President of Ireland, 1959-73. He died in 1975.
13. The Committee included James Murnaghan who was later to become a prominent judge in the new State.

'the Constitution shall be construed with reference to [the Treaty] . . . and if any provision of the said Constitution or any amendment thereof or of any law made thereunder is in any respect repugnant to any of the provisions of the Scheduled Treaty, it shall, to the extent of such repugnancy, be absolutely void and inoperative.'

The Constitution was bound to a Treaty which was opposed, peacefully and with armed force, by a large minority of those under its jurisdiction while being disliked by many reluctant supporters. In cases of conflict, the provisions of that Treaty would supersede the provisions of the Constitution.

Futhermore, although the 1922 Constitution recognised the People as the supreme lawgivers, it contained a dualism repugnant to the republican ideal in that it acknowledged the British Monarch as a constituent part of the legislature (Article 12). The presence of a monarchical entity was an anomaly in what purported to be, by virtue of Article 2, an essentially republican constitution. This dualism was also evident in Article 17, which provided the formula for the oath to be taken by members of the Oireachtas. They were to swear:

'true faith and allegiance to the Constitution of the Irish Free State'

and to be:

'faithful to H.M. King George V, his heirs and successors by law[14]'

---

14. The full text of the oath was as follows:
'I . . . do solemnly swear true faith and allegiance to the Constitution of the Irish Free State as by law established, and that I will be faithful to H.M. King George V, his heirs and successors by law, in virtue of the common citizenship of Ireland with Great Britain and her adherence to and membership of the group of nations forming the British Commonwealth of Nations.'

This oath was to be taken before the Representative of the Crown, or some person nominated by him. The notion of fealty to a state whose constitution declared the people to be the supreme lawgivers was incompatible with the notion of fealty to a monarchical institution.

It is worth noting that it was not necessary to include the Oath of Allegiance in the Constitution. Treaty obligations could have been met equally well by including it in the Standing Orders of the Houses of the Oireachtas, thereby divesting it of a superfluous import. Eamon de Valera maintained that while the Treaty specified that the oath to be taken by members of the Parliament of the Irish Free State would be as prescribed, it had not made the actual taking of the oath a constitutional obligation. He argued that the Government was deliberately retaining the requirement that the oath be sworn as a political means to prevent conscientious republicans from entering the Dáil and he is quoted as paraphrasing a warning once inscribed on the walls of Bandon—'Unionists, Orangemen, anarchists may enter here (i.e. Dáil Éireann) but not a republican.'

Although the presence of the Representative of the Crown was a further instance of the dualism besetting the Constitution, his powers were more nominal than real and were eroded gradually until the passing of the External Relations Act, 1936 which abolished the office of Governor General.[15]

Another crucial Article of the 1922 Constitution was Article 50. This provided for the amendment of the Constitution by the Oireachtas, without reference to the people, for a period of eight years from the date when the Constitution took effect. Article 50 also provided that the following procedure be adopted in relation to amendment after the eight year period expired:

---

15. Of whom there were three: Timothy Healy, 1922-8; James MacNeill, 1928-32; Domhnal O'Buachalla, 1932-7. O'Buachalla agreed to accept the office under the title of Seneschal.

(a) a Bill to amend the Constitution had to be passed by both Houses of the Oireachtas;

(b) the Bill would then be submitted to referendum;

(c) a majority of the electorate would have to have voted;

(d) either a majority of the voters on the electoral register or two-thirds of votes recorded would have to be in favour of the proposed amendment in order to amend.

This would have given the Constitution the rigidity sought by those who drafted it. Before the eight year period expired however, the Amendment No. 16 Act, 1929 (No. 10 of 1929) was passed, extending the period by a further eight years. Thus during its brief existence the Constitution of Saorstát Éireann could be amended by means of ordinary legislation.

Through a series of Amendment Acts, culminating in the Amendment No. 17 Act, 1931 (No. 37 of 1931) personal rights in the 1922 Constitution were whittled down to the minimum. The Amendment No. 17 Act, 1931 inserted Article 2(a) of the Constitution, which gave the Executive Council of the Irish Free State powers of arrest, detention and trial of people before military tribunals not bound by any rules of evidence even though many of the matters triable before these tribunals carried a mandatory death sentence.

The ordinary courts, including the Supreme Court, were unable to interfere with the erosion of personal rights. This became clear during de Valera's reign as President of the Executive Council. In *The State (Ryan) v Lennon*[16], the Supreme Court, albeit with great reluctance on the part of the Chief Justice, arrived at a conclusion which was tantamount to an admission of powerlessness in the face of a situation made possible by Article 2(a).

---

16. 1935 IR 170; 69 ILTR 125.

The process of degeneration was probably inevitable because of the dualist nature of the Constitution which precluded broad acceptance by the people whose charter it purported to be. Furthermore, the Government's manipulation of the Constitution divested it of authority by pushing aside its fundamental doctrines in the interests of pragmatism.

This was exacerbated by the fact that the courts, still under the spell of United Kingdom constitutional principles of parliamentary sovereignty, and inexperienced in their role as protectors of the Constitution, were unable to fulfil the role which the original Constitution implicitly intended them to fulfil.

In the political climate of this period, the renewal of the amendatory power of the Oireachtas was possibly the one factor which, more than any other, stripped the Constitution of Saorstát Éireann of its effectiveness as a source of primary law and robbed it of the promise it held as a model of an enlightened constitution.

In 1932 de Valera's Fianna Fáil party formed a Government[17] and he set about severing the connection with the British Crown. A new Constitution would be an effective means for this process and by 1937 he was ready to present a charter for the Irish People to the Oireachtas and to the people. This charter was to be given to the people by themselves and its legitimacy was to derive from the people alone and from no other source. Having passed through the Oireachtas as a Bill it went to the people rather than to the Crown for ratification. It is not intended to produce an analytical and discursive account of the enactment and amendment of the Constitution of Ireland, rather it is intended by use of their own words to show how the framers of the Constitution (and its subsequent amendment) approached their task.

---

17. Following the general election, the Dáil convened on 9 March 1932 and Mr de Valera was elected President of the Executive Council by 81 votes to 68.

BUNREACHT NA hÉIREANN 1937

The Dáil debates, particularly those covering the Second Stage of the Draft Constitution Bill, provide a useful insight into how the proposed new Constitution was viewed in 1937.

The Second Stage of the Bill was introduced by de Valera in Dáil Éireann on 11 May 1937. In his introductory address to the House, which lasted two and a half hours, he outlined the major provisions of the proposed Constitution. He devoted much time to allaying fears, groundless or real, about the rise of a dictatorship through the medium of the new office of President. It was during this defence of the office of President that de Valera stressed what he considered to be the fundamental attribute of the proposed Constitution. Referring to the right of the people to choose their own form of Government, he said:

> 'If there is one thing more than another that is clear and shining through this whole Constitution, it is the fact that the people are the masters.[18]'

Towards the end of his address, he explained why he considered a new Constitution to be necessary:

> 'I want to repeat what my attitude in regard to the Constitution is. It was clear that a Constitution was necessary and urgently necessary. No people more than the opposition were so insistent in saying that the present position leaves the Government with tremendous powers and without check, and that, in the interests of the community as a whole, it would be better not to leave them these unreasonable powers. Therefore, it is that the Constitution is necessary. It is necessary also from the point of view of bringing to

---

18. Dáil Éireann, Parliamentary Debates, Official Report, 11 May 1937; Column 40.

completion that series of step by step changes which, taken as a whole, have left the old Constitution a tattered and torn affair. The Draft Constitution is, therefore, necessary.[19]'

The proposed Constitution was intended by de Valera to stand on its own and was to derive its authority from no other source than the Irish people, as he declared:

'I do not at this stage want to follow Deputy Costello[20] into another mistaken argument of his that this is an amendment of the old Constitution. It is not. I do not think we could amend the old Constitution in this way. The only way in which you can get a Constitution is to get the people themselves to enact it or get them to elect a Constituent Assembly to enact it . . . Deputy Costello would be telling us that he would have a grand time going to the Supreme Court asking them to say that the Constitution was *ultra vires*. But neither Deputy Costello nor anybody else can tell us that this Draft Constitution is *ultra vires* for it is the people themselves who will enact it. They are the authority . . . This Draft Constitution, if passed at all, is going to be passed by the sovereign people who are above the lawyers and above Government and all others. Their will is the final decision and once they have voted on it and their elected representatives come together this Draft becomes, in accordance with its own terms, law within a certain date . . . This is a new Constitution put before the people and the people will enact it with such amendments as we may make here. When it is enacted it is the foundation law of the sovereign people of this country and, I therefore put it before the Dáil.[21]'

19. Ibid. Col. 73.
20. John A. Costello: Born in 1881; Attorney General, 1926-32; Taoiseach, 1948-51 and 1954-7.
21. Ibid. Col. 74.

In moving rejection of the Draft, Deputy Frank MacDermot stated:

> 'I find myself in a somewhat peculiar position in moving the rejection of this Constitution, because, except in so far as it affects our relations with the other nations of the British Commonwealth and our relations with Northern Ireland, I like this Constitution. I find that the greater part of it commands not merely my support, but my warm support. I think that the bulk of the criticisms that have been directed against it have been misconceived.[22]'

MacDermot did not see that the fears regarding the possibility of Presidential dictatorship, which had been widely expressed outside Dáil Éireann, had any real basis and having referred to comment in the press, both at home and abroad, he said that enthusiastic friends may be just as responsible for certain misunderstandings as interested and hostile critics.[23]

He was much more worried about the possible effect of the proposed Constitution on the achievement of unity with Northern Ireland, and thought that:

> 'the Government, in this draft Constitution, have misused a great opportunity . . . that problem [i.e. partition] can only be solved by inducing the Northern Unionists to give their first allegiance to Ireland. For this to be possible, we have got to offer them an Ireland in which a place can be found for their traditions and aspirations as well as for ours. Until we are willing to do this we are partitionist at heart, no matter how loudly we shout about unity. The six Northern counties will

22. Ibid. Col. 77.
23. Ibid. Col. 78.

have no part in the coming plebiscite on these constitutional proposals.[24']

He went on to refer to the place of the British Monarch in the proposed new order of things:

> 'the first great fault of these proposals is the omission of the King except in so far as he survives, precariously, as an organ or instrument for external use only.[25']

MacDermot also bemoaned the failure to 'make an open declaration of our membership of the Commonwealth',[26] while at the same time noting that:

> 'Once again our republicans have abstained from declaring a republic . . . To declare a republic for the whole of Éire would be no greater an excursion into the realms of unreality than to do what this Constitution purports to do.[27']

While he thought that the provisions of the Draft Constitution relating to the special position of the Catholic Church 'were entirely without meaning',[28] MacDermot referred to comments in the *Irish Independent* by Professor Berriedale Keith that this provision was the one most likely to obstruct union, and said that:

> 'I can hardly attach much importance to it, because I do not perceive that it has any practical implications. But certainly it would be better absent as far as partition is concerned.[29']

24. Ibid. Col. 10.
25. Ibid. Col. 80.
26. Ibid. Col. 81.
27. Ibid. Col. 81.
28. Ibid. Col. 82.
29. Ibid. Col. 82.

Professor Alton, in formally seconding Deputy MacDermot said:

> 'I may say, too, that I agree with most of Deputy MacDermot's remarks about the Constitution, that it is a well-framed, well-balanced, equitable piece of work, thoroughly democratic, broadbased on the people's will, but it is rather lamentable that our future relations with the North should remain in this ambiguous position.[30]'

General Mulcahy, in the course of moving postponement, said that the Government would be far better employed in addressing the country's economic problems than introducing a Constitution. He said:

> 'I want this proposal postponed in this House because, during this month, we should have the attention of the Government, the Dáil and of our people concentrated in an undivided way on critical matters affecting the economic present, and particularly, the economic future of our people.[31]'

The Deputy continued, mainly on the subject of the economic ills which beset the country and advocating a Canadian–type trade agreement with the United Kingdom.

Deputy Daniel Morrissey seconded General Mulcahy's motion saying:

> 'I would like at the outset to say that I am not terribly concerned about this Constitution. There are matters that are much more urgent, much more important and of much more concern to the people of this country than the Draft of the Constitution that we have before

30. Ibid. Col. 84.
31. Ibid. Col. 90.

us today . . . The President, of course, realises now what everybody in the country knows that the country is not interested in this Constitution. The people are not concerned with it . . . The President was not even able to hold the attention of the members of his own party.[32]'

Like General Mulcahy, Deputy Morrissey expressed more concern with economic issues, and saw the proposed Constitution as having little relevance, as his remarks regarding those provisions which affected women show:

'The President tells us that 99 per cent of the women would agree with this Constitution if they read and understood it. Let me tell him that 99 per cent of the women and children are more concerned with the price of flour than they are with this Constitution. That aspect presents a graver problem to them, and there is nothing in this Constitution that is going to give one loaf extra to any family in this country.[33]'

Later, on the subject of unemployment, he said:

'We are expected . . . to give our time to this Constitution, to take it seriously and give serious debate to it. Will the President at some future time—he did not in his two and a half hours' speech—tell this country what is in this Constitution that is going to reduce the number of unemployed below 100,000? . . . But it is easier for the President and his Ministers to talk about Constitutions than it is to face up to hard facts, to questions of economics, to face up to the question of solving the unemployment problem.[34]'

---

32. Ibid. Cols. 98-9.
33. Ibid. Col. 101.
34. Ibid. Cols. 101-2.

From within the ranks of the Fianna Fáil Party the problem of partition was raised. Deputy Eamon Donnelly, seconded by Deputy Thomas Hales,[35] sought to have the Second Reading postponed pending the reunification of the country, so that the Constitution could be submitted to the people of the entire island.[36]

Deputy Lavery, having deplored the lack of consultation during the preparation of the Draft, was concerned to point out to the House that the new Constitution might be 'a serious source of danger' if it were to be enacted. The first point he raised, dealt with the nature of Constitutions and the specific problem with this Constitution:

> 'I think it will be generally agreed that the Constitution ought to be a simple, straightforward statement of the fundamental law and that it ought to deal as briefly and as succinctly as possible with the fundamentals of the law of the State: that it ought not to go further; that it ought not to be an essay on social policy or a statement of ideals; or that it ought not to state matters in detail regarding the ordinary rights of citizens with regard to the ordinary law . . . Now, we have here a Draft Constitution of something like 60 Articles, consisting of some Articles, which, certainly, could not be considered or applied in any ordinary court of law because of their vagueness and generality.[37]'

He went on to deal with various aspects of the Draft and in the course of his address he provided the House with his general view of it:

> 'apart from certain pronouncements on social policy which it necessarily contains, the only important feature

---

35. Ibid. Cols. 118-24.
36. Ibid. Cols. 104-18.
37. Ibid. Cols. 126-7.

of the new Constitution is this new position of President.
I do not think it is an improvement.[38]'

Professor O'Sullivan expressed the fear that the office of
President would lead to a dictatorship.[39] He, and others, also
expressed concern that the Constitution would reduce
women's rights because, for instance, it did not specifically
recognise their right to vote.

Deputy Helena Concannon, although concerned with the
issue of the diminution of women's rights under the
proposed Constitution, said of Article 45 of the Draft Bill:

> 'the nervous system of women needs to be specially
> protected, and I think that Article 45, which gives them
> a constitutional right to that protection, should not be
> interfered with.[40]'

and of Article 41 'I sincerely hope that not a comma of this
noble declaration will be altered'.

Deputy John A. Costello repeated his claim that the Draft
Constitution was an amendment to the old Constitution and
articulated grave fears about the office of President:

> 'The scheme is one for dictatorial powers, come what
> may, to whoever is President, whether it is the present
> President of the Executive Council or somebody else
> . . . I tell the House there is not a greater tyranny than
> the tyranny which masquerades under the cloak of
> democracy. That is the sort of tyranny that is
> embodied in that document before the House, a
> tyranny which masquerades under the cloak of
> democracy.[41]'

---

38. Ibid. Col. 131.
39. Official Report, 12 May 1937, Col. 210-39.
40. Ibid. Col. 246.
41. Ibid. Col. 303.

Deputy Costello was also concerned with the prospect of a diminution of women's rights:

> 'in my opinion, there are inherent defects in these provisions of the Draft Constitution with regard to the status of women.[42]'

The foregoing very brief extracts from the extensive Dáil Debates give a general flavour of the attitudes displayed towards the Draft Constitution in the Dáil. The debate itself dealt with the Draft in great detail and a careful reading of the Dáil Debates is necessary to understand the nuances of opinion involved.

On 25 May 1937 the Plebiscite (Draft Constitution) Bill, 1937 was introduced in the Dáil and the Second Stage was ordered for 1 June. The 25 May also saw the beginning of the Committee Stage of the Draft Constitution Bill.

The Draft Constitution Bill was recommitted to a Committee of the entire House on 9 June 1937 in respect of amendments and on 14 June 1937 the final stage of the Bill was moved in the House. The Dáil divided—sixty-two in favour and forty-eight against—and the motion was declared carried. De Valera announced that the referendum and general election would take place on 1 July 1937.

Total electorate		1,775,055
Total poll		1,346,207
Percentage poll		75.8%
Votes in favour	685,105	[56.52%]
Votes against	526,945	[43.48%]
Spoiled votes		134,157

In the referendum the Bill was carried by a majority of 56.52 per cent. It was carried in all but five of the thirty-four Borough and County constituencies. The Constitution came into operation on 29 December 1937.

---

42. Ibid. Col. 314.

The Collated Text of the Constitution

Bunreacht na hÉireann

PREAMBLE

In the name of the Most Holy Trinity, from Whom is all authority and to Whom, as our final end, all actions both of men and States must be referred,

We, the people of Éire,

Humbly acknowledging all our obligations to our Divine Lord, Jesus Christ, Who sustained our fathers through centuries of trial,

Gratefully remembering their heroic and unremitting struggle to regain the rightful independence of our Nation,

And seeking to promote the common good, with due observance of Prudence, Justice and Charity, so that the dignity and freedom of the individual may be assured, true social order attained, the unity of our country restored, and concord established with other nations,

Do hereby adopt, enact, and give to ourselves this Constitution.

THE NATION.

Article 1.

The Irish nation hereby affirms its inalienable, indefeasible, and sovereign right to choose its own form of Government, to determine its relations with other nations, and to develop its life, political, economic and cultural, in accordance with its own genius and traditions.

THE NATION.

Article 2.

The national territory consists of the whole island of Ireland, its islands and the territorial seas.

THE NATION.

Article 3.

Pending the re-integration of the national territory, and without prejudice to the right of the Parliament and Government established by this Constitution to exercise jurisdiction over the whole of that territory, the laws enacted by that Parliament shall have the like area and extent of application as the laws of Saorstát Éireann and the like extra-territorial effect.

THE STATE.

Article 4.

The name of the State is Éire, or, in the English language, *Ireland*.

THE STATE.

Article 5.

Ireland is a sovereign, independent, democratic state.

THE STATE.

Article 6.

1. All powers of government, legislative, executive and judicial, derive, under God, from the people, whose right it is to designate the rulers of the State and, in final appeal, to decide all questions of national policy, according to the requirements of the common good.

2. These powers of government are exercisable only by or on the authority of the organs of State established by this Constitution.

THE STATE.

Article 7.
The national flag is the tricolour of green, white and orange.

THE STATE.

Article 8.

1. The Irish language as the national language is the first official language.

2. The English language is recognised as a second official language.

3. Provision may, however, be made by law for the exclusive use of either of the said languages for any one or more official purposes, either throughout the State or in any part thereof.

THE STATE.

Article 9.

1. 1° On the coming into operation of this Constitution any person who was a citizen of Saorstát Éireann immediately before the coming into operation of this Constitution shall become and be a citizen of Ireland.

   2° The future acquisition and loss of Irish nationality and citizenship shall be determined in accordance with law.

   3° No person may be excluded from Irish nationality and citizenship by reason of the sex of such person.

2. Fidelity to the nation and loyalty to the State are fundamental political duties of all citizens.

THE STATE.

Article 10.

1. All natural resources, including the air and all forms of potential energy, within the jurisdiction of the Parliament and Government established by this Constitution and all royalties and franchises within that jurisdiction belong to the State subject to all estates and interests therein for the time being lawfully vested in any person or body.

2. All land and all mines, minerals and waters which belonged to Saorstát Éireann immediately before the coming into operation of this Constitution belong to the State to the same extent as they then belonged to Saorstát Éireann.

Article 10 *(contd.)*

3. Provision may be made by law for the management of the property which belongs to the State by virtue of this Article and for the control of the alienation, whether temporary or permanent, of that property.

4. Provision may also be made by law for the management of land, mines, minerals and waters acquired by the State after the coming into operation of this Constitution and for the control of the alienation, whether temporary or permanent, of the land, mines, minerals and waters so acquired.

THE STATE.

Article 11.

All revenues of the State from whatever source arising shall, subject to such exception as may be provided by law, form one fund, and shall be appropriated for the purposes and in the manner and subject to the charges and liabilities determined and imposed by law.

THE PRESIDENT.

Article 12.

1. There shall be a President of Ireland (*Uachtarán na hÉireann*), hereinafter called the President, who shall take precedence over all other persons in the State and who shall exercise and perform the powers and functions conferred on the President by this Constitution and by law.

2. 1° The President shall be elected by direct vote of the people.

   2° Every citizen who has the right to vote at an election for members of Dáil Éireann shall have the right to vote at an election for President.

Article 12 *(contd.)*

3°   The voting shall be by secret ballot and on the system of proportional representation by means of the single transferable vote.

3. 1°   The President shall hold office for seven years from the date upon which he enters upon his office, unless before the expiration of that period he dies, or resigns, or is removed from office, or becomes permanently incapacitated, such incapacity being established to the satisfaction of the Supreme Court consisting of not less than five judges.

2°   A person who holds, or who has held, office as President, shall be eligible for re-election to that office once, but only once.

3°   An election for the office of President shall be held not later than, and not earlier than the sixtieth day before, the date of the expiration of the term of office of every President, but in the event of the removal from office of the President or of his death, resignation, or permanent incapacity established as aforesaid (whether occurring before or after he enters upon his office)[43], an election for the office of President shall be held within sixty days after such event.

4. 1°   Every citizen who has reached his thirty-fifth year of age is eligible for election to the office of President.

2°   Every candidate for election, not a former or retiring President, must be nominated either by:

i.   not less than twenty persons, each of whom is at the time a member of one of the Houses of the Oireachtas, or

43. Second Amendment of the Constitution Act, 1941, Ref. No. 2.

Article 12 *(contd.)*

> ii. by the Councils of not less than four administrative Counties (including County Boroughs) as defined by law.

3° No person and no such Council shall be entitled to subscribe to the nomination of more than one candidate in respect of the same election.

4° Former or retiring Presidents may become candidates on their own nomination.

5° Where only one candidate is nominated for the office of President it shall not be necessary to proceed to a ballot for his election.

5. Subject to the provisions of this Article, elections for the office of President shall be regulated by law.

6. 1° The President shall not be a member of either House of the Oireachtas.

   2° If a member of either House of the Oireachtas be elected President, he shall be deemed to have vacated his seat in that House.

   3° The President shall not hold any other office or position of emolument.

7. The first President shall enter upon his office as soon as may be after his election, and every subsequent President shall enter upon his office on the day following the expiration of the term of office of his predecessor or as soon as may be thereafter or, in the event of his predecessor's removal from office, death, resignation, or

Article 12 *(contd.)*

permanent incapacity established as provided by section 3 hereof, as soon as may be after the election.

8. The President shall enter upon his office by taking and subscribing publicly, in the presence of members of both Houses of the Oireachtas, of Judges of the Supreme Court and of the High Court, and other public personages, the following declaration:—

> "In the presence of Almighty God I
> do solemnly and sincerely promise and declare that I will maintain the Constitution of Ireland and uphold its laws, that I will fulfil my duties faithfully and conscientiously in accordance with the Constitution and the law, and that I will dedicate my abilities to the service and welfare of the people of Ireland. May God direct and sustain me."

9. The President shall not leave the State during his term of office save with the consent of the Government.

10. 1° The President may be impeached for stated misbehaviour.

    2° The charge shall be preferred by either of the Houses of the Oireachtas, subject to and in accordance with the provisions of this section.

    3° A proposal to either House of the Oireachtas to prefer a charge against the President under this section shall not be entertained unless upon a notice of motion in writing signed by not less than thirty members of that House.

Article 12 *(contd.)*

4° No such proposal shall be adopted by either of the Houses of the Oireachtas save upon a resolution of that House supported by not less than two-thirds of the total membership thereof.

5° When a charge has been preferred by either House of the Oireachtas, the other House shall investigate the charge, or cause the charge to be investigated.

6° The President shall have the right to appear and to be represented at the investigation of the charge.

7° If, as a result of the investigation, a resolution be passed supported by not less than two-thirds of the total membership of the House of the Oireachtas by which the charge was investigated, or caused to be investigated, declaring that the charge preferred against the President has been sustained and that the misbehaviour, the subject of the charge, was such as to render him unfit to continue in office, such resolution shall operate to remove the President from his office.

11. 1° The President shall have an official residence in or near the City of Dublin.

2° The President shall receive such emoluments and allowances as may be determined by law.

3° The emoluments and allowances of the President shall not be diminished during his term of office.

THE PRESIDENT.

Article 13.

1. 1° The President shall, on the nomination of Dáil Éireann, appoint the Taoiseach, that is, the head of the Government or Prime Minister.

    2° The President shall, on the nomination of the Taoiseach with the previous approval of Dáil Éireann, appoint the other members of the Government.

    3° The President shall, on the advice of the Taoiseach, accept the resignation or terminate the appointment of any member of the Government.

Article 13 *(contd.)*

2. 1° Dáil Éireann shall be summoned and dissolved by the President on the advice of the Taoiseach.

    2° The President may in his absolute discretion refuse to dissolve Dáil Éireann on the advice of a Taoiseach who has ceased to retain the support of a majority in Dáil Éireann.

    3° The President may at any time, after consultation with the Council of State, convene a meeting of either or both of the Houses of the Oireachtas.

3. 1° Every Bill passed or deemed to have been passed by both Houses of the Oireachtas shall require the signature of the President for its enactment into law.

    2° The President shall promulgate every law made by the Oireachtas.

4. The supreme command of the Defence Forces is hereby vested in the President.

5. 1° The exercise of the supreme command of the Defence Forces shall be regulated by law.

    2° All commissioned officers of the Defence Forces shall hold their commissions from the President.

6. The right of pardon and the power to commute or remit punishment imposed by any court exercising criminal jurisdiction are hereby vested in the President, but such power of commutation or remission may, except in capital cases, also be conferred by law on other authorities.

Article 13 *(contd.)*

7. 1° The President may, after consultation with the Council of State, communicate with the Houses of the Oireachtas by message or address on any matter of national or public importance.

   2° The President may, after consultation with the Council of State, address a message to the Nation at any time on any such matter.

   3° Every such message or address must, however, have received the approval of the Government.

8. 1° The President shall not be answerable to either House of the Oireachtas or to any court for the exercise and performance of the powers and functions of his office or for any act done or purporting to be done by him in the exercise and performance of these powers and functions.

   2° The behaviour of the President may, however, be brought under review in either of the Houses of the Oireachtas for the purposes of section 10 of Article 12 of this Constitution, or by any court, tribunal or body appointed or designated by either of the Houses of the Oireachtas for the investigation of a charge under section 10 of the said Article.

9. The powers and functions conferred on the President by this Constitution shall be exercisable and performable by him only on the advice of the Government, save where it is provided by this Constitution that he shall act in his absolute discretion or after consultation with or in relation to the Council of State, or on the advice or nomination of, or on receipt of any other communication from, any other person or body.

Article 13 *(contd.)*

10. Subject to this Constitution, additional powers and functions may be conferred on the President by law.

11. No power or function conferred on the President by law shall be exercisable or performable by him save only on the advice of the Government.

THE PRESIDENT.

Article 14.

1. In the event of the absence of the President, or his temporary incapacity, or his permanent incapacity established as provided by section 3 of Article 12 hereof, or in the event of his death, resignation, removal from office, or failure to exercise and perform the powers and functions of his office or any of them, or at any time at which the office of President may be vacant, the powers and functions conferred on the President ~~by this Constitution~~ by or under this Constitution[44] shall be exercised and performed by a Commission constituted as provided in section 2 of this Article.

---

44. Second Amendment of the Constitution Act, 1941, Ref. No. 4.

Article 14 *(contd.)*

2. 1° The Commission shall consist of the following persons, namely, the Chief Justice, the Chairman of Dáil Éireann (An Ceann Comhairle), and the Chairman of Seanad Éireann.

   2° The President of the High Court shall act as a member of the Commission in the place of the Chief Justice on any occasion on which the office of Chief Justice is vacant or on which the Chief Justice is unable to act.

   3° The Deputy Chairman of Dáil Éireann shall act as a member of the Commission in the place of the Chairman of Dáil Éireann on any occasion on which the office of Chairman of Dáil Éireann is vacant or on which the said Chairman is unable to act.

   4° The Deputy Chairman of Seanad Éireann shall act as a member of the Commission in the place of the Chairman of Seanad Éireann on any occasion on which the office of Chairman of Seanad Éireann is vacant or on which the said Chairman is unable to act.

3. The Commission may act by any two of their number and may act notwithstanding a vacancy in their membership.

4. The Council of State may by a majority of its members make such provision as to them may seem meet for the exercise and performance of the powers and functions conferred on the President ~~by this Constitution~~ by or under this Constitution[45] in any contingency which is not provided for by the foregoing provisions of this Article.

---

45. Second Amendment of the Constitution Act, 1941, Ref. No. 4.

Article 14 *(contd.)*

5. 1° The provisions of this Constitution which relate to the exercise and performance by the President of the powers and functions conferred on him ~~by this Constitution~~ by or under this Constitution[46] shall subject to the subsequent provisions of this section apply to the exercise and performance of the said powers and functions under this Article.

   2° In the event of the failure of the President to exercise or perform any power or function which the President is ~~by this Constitution~~ by or under this Constitution[47] required to exercise or perform within a specified time, the said power or function shall be exercised or performed under this Article, as soon as may be after the expiration of the time so specified.

46. Second Amendment of the Constitution Act, 1941, Ref. No. 4.
47. Second Amendment of the Constitution Act, 1941, Ref. No. 4.

THE NATIONAL PARLIAMENT.

Constitution and Powers.

Article 15.

1. 1° The National Parliament shall be called and known, and is in this Constitution generally referred to, as the Oireachtas.

   2° The Oireachtas shall consist of the President and two Houses, viz.: a House of Representatives to be called Dáil Éireann and a Senate to be called Seanad Éireann.

   3° The Houses of the Oireachtas shall sit in or near the City of Dublin or in such other place as they may from time to time determine.

Article 15 *(contd.)*

2. 1° The sole and exclusive power of making laws for the State is hereby vested in the Oireachtas: no other legislative authority has power to make laws for the State.

    2° Provision may however be made by law for the creation or recognition of subordinate legislatures and for the powers and functions of these legislatures.

3. 1° The Oireachtas may provide for the establishment or recognition of functional or vocational councils representing branches of the social and economic life of the people.

    2° A law establishing or recognising any such council shall determine its rights, powers and duties, and its relation to the Oireachtas and to the Government.

4. 1° The Oireachtas shall not enact any law which is in any respect repugnant to this Constitution or any provision thereof.

    2° Every law enacted by the Oireachtas which is in any respect repugnant to this Constitution or to any provision thereof, shall, but to the extent only of such repugnancy, be invalid.

5. The Oireachtas shall not declare acts to be infringements of the law which were not so at the date of their commission.

6. 1° The right to raise and maintain military or armed forces is vested exclusively in the Oireachtas.

Article 15 *(contd.)*

2° No military or armed force, other than a military or armed force raised and maintained by the Oireachtas, shall be raised or maintained for any purpose whatsoever.

7. The Oireachtas shall hold at least one session every year.

8. 1° Sittings of each House of the Oireachtas shall be public.

2° In cases of special emergency, however, either House may hold a private sitting with the assent of two-thirds of the members present.

9. 1° Each House of the Oireachtas shall elect from its members its own Chairman and Deputy Chairman, and shall prescribe their powers and duties.

2° The remuneration of the Chairman and Deputy Chairman of each House shall be determined by law.

10. Each House shall make its own rules and standing orders, with power to attach penalties for their infringement, and shall have power to ensure freedom of debate, to protect its official documents and the private papers of its members, and to protect itself and its members against any person or persons interfering with, molesting or attempting to corrupt its members in the exercise of their duties.

11. 1° All questions in each House shall, save as otherwise provided by this Constitution, be determined by a majority of the votes of the members present and voting other than the Chairman or presiding member.

Article 15 *(contd.)*

2° The Chairman or presiding member shall have and exercise a casting vote in the case of an equality of votes.

3° The number of members necessary to constitute a meeting of either House for the exercise of its powers shall be determined by its standing orders.

12. All official reports and publications of the Oireachtas or of either House thereof and utterances made in either House wherever published shall be privileged.

13. The members of each House of the Oireachtas shall, except in case of treason as defined in this Constitution, felony or breach of the peace, be privileged from arrest in going to and returning from, and while within the precincts of, either House, and shall not, in respect of any utterance in either House, be amenable to any court or any authority other than the House itself.

14. No person may be at the same time a member of both Houses of the Oireachtas, and, if any person who is already a member of either House becomes a member of the other House, he shall forthwith be deemed to have vacated his first seat.

15. The Oireachtas may make provision by law for the payment of allowances to the members of each House thereof in respect of their duties as public representatives and for the grant to them of free travelling and such other facilities (if any) in connection with those duties as the Oireachtas may determine.

THE NATIONAL PARLIAMENT.

Dáil Éireann.

Article 16.

1. 1° Every citizen without distinction of sex who has reached the age of twenty-one years, and who is not placed under disability or incapacity by this Constitution or by law, shall be eligible for membership of Dáil Éireann.

   2° ~~Every citizen without distinction of sex who has reached the age of twenty-one years~~ eighteen years[48] ~~who is not disqualified by law and complies with the provisions of the law relating to the election of members of Dáil Éireann, shall have the right to vote at an election for members of Dáil Éireann.~~[49]

---

48. Fourth Amendment of the Constitution Act, 1972.
49. Ninth Amendment of the Constitution Act, 1984.

Article 16 *(contd.)*

2° i. All citizens, and

  ii. such other persons in the State as may be determined by law,

without distinction of sex who have reached the age of eighteen years who are not disqualified by law and comply with the provisions of the law relating to the election of members of Dáil Éireann, shall have the right to vote at an election for members of Dáil Éireann.[49]

3° No law shall be enacted placing any citizen under disability or incapacity for membership of Dáil Éireann on the ground of sex or disqualifying any citizen or other person[50] from voting at an election for members of Dáil Éireann on that ground.

4° No voter may exercise more than one vote at an election for Dáil Éireann, and the voting shall be by secret ballot.

2. 1° Dáil Éireann shall be composed of members who represent constituencies determined by law.

  2° The number of members shall from time to time be fixed by law but the total number of members of Dáil Éireann shall not be fixed at less than one member for each thirty thousand of the population, or at more than one member for each twenty thousand of the population.

  3° The ratio between the number of members to be elected at any time for each constituency and the population of each constituency, as ascertained at

49. Ninth Amendment of the Constitution Act, 1984.
50. Ninth Amendment of the Constitution Act, 1984.

Article 16 *(contd.)*

the last preceding census, shall, so far as it is practicable, be the same throughout the country.

4° The Oireachtas shall revise the constituencies at least once in every twelve years, with due regard to changes in distribution of the population, but any alterations in the constituencies shall not take effect during the life of Dáil Éireann sitting when such revision is made.

5° The members shall be elected on the system of proportional representation by means of the single transferable vote.

6° No law shall be enacted whereby the number of members to be returned for any constituency shall be less than three.

3. 1° Dáil Éireann shall be summoned and dissolved as provided by section 2 of Article 13 of this Constitution.

2° A general election for members of Dáil Éireann shall take place not later than thirty days after a dissolution of Dáil Éireann.

4. 1° Polling at every general election for Dáil Éireann shall as far as practicable take place on the same day throughout the country.

2° Dáil Éireann shall meet within thirty days from that polling day.

Article 16 *(contd.)*

5. The same Dáil Éireann shall not continue for a longer
   period than seven years from the date of its first meeting:
   a shorter period may be fixed by law.

6. Provision shall be made by law to enable the member of
   Dáil Éireann who is the Chairman immediately before a
   dissolution of Dáil Éireann to be deemed without any
   actual election to be elected a member of Dáil Éireann at
   the ensuing general election.

7. Subject to the foregoing provisions of this Article,
   elections for membership of Dáil Éireann, including the
   filling of casual vacancies, shall be regulated in
   accordance with law.

THE NATIONAL PARLIAMENT.

Dáil Éireann.

Article 17.

1. 1° As soon as possible after the presentation to Dáil Éireann under Article 28 of this Constitution of the Estimates of receipts and the Estimates of expenditure of the State for any financial year, Dáil Éireann shall consider such Estimates.

   2° Save in so far as may be provided by specific enactment in each case, the legislation required to give effect to the Financial Resolutions of each year shall be enacted within that year.

Article 17 *(contd.)*

2. Dáil Éireann shall not pass any vote or resolution, and no law shall be enacted, for the appropriation of revenue or other public moneys unless the purpose of the appropriation shall have been recommended to Dáil Éireann by a message from the Government signed by the Taoiseach.

THE NATIONAL PARLIAMENT.

Seanad Éireann.

Article 18.

1. Seanad Éireann shall be composed of sixty members, of whom eleven shall be nominated members and forty-nine shall be elected members.

2. A person to be eligible for membership of Seanad Éireann must be eligible to become a member of Dáil Éireann.

3. The nominated members of Seanad Éireann shall be ~~nominated by the Taoiseach with their prior consent~~ nominated, with their prior consent, by the Taoiseach who is appointed next after the re-assembly of Dáil Éireann following the dissolution thereof which occasions the nomination of the said members.[51]

---

51. Second Amendment of the Constitution Act, 1941, Ref. No. 6.

Article 18 *(contd.)*

4. 1° The elected members of Seanad Éireann shall be elected as follows:—

> i.   Three shall be elected by the National University of Ireland.
>
> ii. Three shall be elected by the University of Dublin.
>
> iii. Forty-three shall be elected from panels of candidates constituted as hereinafter provided.

2° Provision may be made by law for the election, on a franchise and in the manner to be provided by law, by one or more of the following institutions, namely:

> i.   the universities mentioned in subsection 1° of this section,
>
> ii. any other institutions of higher education in the State, of so many members of Seanad Éireann as may be fixed by law in substitution for an equal number of the members to be elected pursuant to paragraphs i and ii of the said subsection 1°.

A member or members of Seanad Éireann may be elected under this subsection by institutions grouped together or by a single institution.

3° Nothing in this Article shall be invoked to prohibit the dissolution by law of a university mentioned in subsection 1° of this section.[52]

---

52. Seventh Amendment of the Constitution Act, 1979.

Article 18 *(contd.)*

5. Every election of the elected members of Seanad Éireann shall be held on the system of proportional representation by means of the single transferable vote, and by secret postal ballot.

6. The members of Seanad Éireann to be elected by the Universities shall be elected on a franchise and in the manner to be provided by law.

7. 1° Before each general election of the members of Seanad Éireann to be elected from panels of candidates, five panels of candidates shall be formed in the manner provided by law containing respectively the names of persons having knowledge and practical experience of the following interests and services, namely:—

    i.   National Language and Culture, Literature, Art, Education and such professional interests as may be defined by law for the purpose of this panel;

    ii.   Agriculture and allied interests, and Fisheries;

    iii.   Labour, whether organised or unorganised;

    iv.   Industry and Commerce, including banking, finance, accountancy, engineering and architecture;

    v.   Public Administration and social services, including voluntary social activities.

  2° Not more than eleven and, subject to the provisions of Article 19 hereof, not less than five members of Seanad Éireann shall be elected from any one panel.

Article 18 *(contd.)*

8. A general election for Seanad Éireann shall take place not later than ninety days after a dissolution of Dáil Éireann, and the first meeting of Seanad Éireann after the general election shall take place on a day to be fixed by the President on the advice of the Taoiseach.

9. Every member of Seanad Éireann shall, unless he previously dies, resigns, or becomes disqualified, continue to hold office until the day before the polling day of the general election for Seanad Éireann next held after his election or nomination.

10. 1° Subject to the foregoing provisions of this Article elections of the elected members of Seanad Éireann shall be regulated by law.

2° Casual vacancies in the number of the nominated members of Seanad Éireann shall be filled by nomination by the Taoiseach with the prior consent of persons so nominated.

3° Casual vacancies in the number of the elected members of Seanad Éireann shall be filled in the manner provided by law.

THE NATIONAL PARLIAMENT.

Seanad Éireann.

Article 19.

Provision may be made by law for the direct election by any functional or vocational group or association or council of so many members of Seanad Éireann as may be fixed by such law in substitution for an equal number of the members to be elected from the corresponding panels of candidates constituted under Article 18 of this Constitution.

THE NATIONAL PARLIAMENT.

Legislation.

Article 20.

1. Every Bill initiated in and passed by Dáil Éireann shall be sent to Seanad Éireann and may, unless it be a Money Bill, be amended in Seanad Éireann and Dáil Éireann shall consider any such amendment.

2. 1° A Bill other than a Money Bill may be initiated in Seanad Éireann, and if passed by Seanad Éireann, shall be introduced in Dáil Éireann.

   2° A Bill initiated in Seanad Éireann if amended in Dáil Éireann shall be considered as a Bill initiated in Dáil Éireann.

3. A Bill passed by either House and accepted by the other House shall be deemed to have been passed by both Houses.

THE NATIONAL PARLIAMENT.

Legislation.

Money Bills.

Article 21.

1. 1° Money Bills shall be initiated in Dáil Éireann only.

    2° Every Money Bill passed by Dáil Éireann shall be sent to Seanad Éireann for its recommendations.

2. 1° Every Money Bill sent to Seanad Éireann for its recommendations shall, at the expiration of a period not longer than twenty-one days after it shall have been sent to Seanad Éireann, be returned to Dáil Éireann, which may accept or reject all or any of the recommendations of Seanad Éireann.

Article 21 *(contd.)*

2° If such Money Bill is not returned by Seanad Éireann to Dáil Éireann within such twenty-one days or is returned within such twenty-one days with recommendations which Dáil Éireann does not accept, it shall be deemed to have been passed by both Houses at the expiration of the said twenty-one days.

THE NATIONAL PARLIAMENT.

Legislation.

Money Bills.

Article 22.

1. 1° A Money Bill means a Bill which contains only
    provisions dealing with all or any of the following
    matters, namely, the imposition, repeal, remission,
    alteration or regulation of taxation; the imposition
    for the payment of debt or other financial purposes
    of charges on public moneys or the variation or
    repeal of any such charges; supply; the
    appropriation, receipt, custody, issue or audit of
    accounts of public money; the raising or guarantee of
    any loan or the repayment thereof; matters
    subordinate and incidental to these matters or any of
    them.

Article 22 *(contd.)*

2° In this definition the expressions "taxation", "public money" and "loan" respectively do not include any taxation, money or loan raised by local authorities or bodies for local purposes.

2. 1° The Chairman of Dáil Éireann shall certify any Bill which, in his opinion, is a Money Bill to be a Money Bill, and his certificate shall, subject to the subsequent provisions of this section, be final and conclusive.

2° Seanad Éireann, by a resolution, passed at a sitting at which not less than thirty members are present, may request the President to refer the question whether the Bill is or is not a Money Bill to a Committee of Privileges.

3° If the President after consultation with the Council of State decided to accede to the request he shall appoint a Committee of Privileges consisting of an equal number of members of Dáil Éireann and of Seanad Éireann and a Chairman who shall be a Judge of the Supreme Court: these appointments shall be made after consultation with the Council of State. In the case of an equality of votes but not otherwise the Chairman shall be entitled to vote.

4° The President shall refer the question to the Committee of Privileges so appointed and the Committee shall report its decision thereon to the President within twenty-one days after the day on which the Bill was sent to Seanad Éireann.

5° The decision of the Committee shall be final and conclusive.

Article 22 *(contd.)*

6° If the President after consultation with the Council of
State decides not to accede to the request of Seanad
Éireann, or if the Committee of Privileges fails to
report within the time hereinbefore specified the
certificate of the Chairman of Dáil Éireann shall stand
confirmed.

THE NATIONAL PARLIAMENT.

Legislation.

Time for Consideration of Bills.

Article 23.

1. This Article applies to every Bill passed by Dáil Éireann and sent to Seanad Éireann other than a Money Bill or a Bill the time for the consideration of which by Seanad Éireann shall have been abridged under Article 24 of this Constitution.

   1° Whenever a Bill to which this Article applies is within the stated period defined in the next following sub-section either rejected by Seanad Éireann or passed by Seanad Éireann with amendments to which Dáil Éireann does not agree or is neither passed (with or without amendment) nor rejected by Seanad Éireann within the stated period, the Bill shall, if Dáil Éireann so resolves within one

Article 23 *(contd.)*

hundred and eighty days after the expiration of the stated period be deemed to have been passed by both Houses of the Oireachtas on the day on which the resolution is passed.

2° The stated period is the period of ninety days commencing on the day on which the Bill is first sent by Dáil Éireann to Seanad Éireann or any longer period agreed upon in respect of the Bill by both Houses of the Oireachtas.

2. 1° The preceding section of this Article shall apply to a Bill which is initiated in and passed by Seanad Éireann, amended by Dáil Éireann, and accordingly deemed to have been initiated in Dáil Éireann.

2° For the purpose of this application the stated period shall in relation to such a Bill commence on the day on which the Bill is first sent to Seanad Éireann after having been amended by Dáil Éireann.

THE NATIONAL PARLIAMENT.

Legislation.

Time for Consideration of Bills.

Article 24.

1. If and whenever on the passage by Dáil Éireann of any Bill, other than a Bill expressed to be a Bill containing a proposal to amend the Constitution, the Taoiseach certifies by messages in writing addressed to the President and to the Chairman of each House of the Oireachtas that, in the opinion of the Government, the Bill is urgent and immediately necessary for the preservation of the public peace and security, or by reason of the existence of a public emergency, whether domestic or international, the time for the consideration of such Bill by Seanad Éireann shall, if Dáil Éireann so resolves and if the President, after consultation with the Council of State, concurs, be abridged to such period as shall be specified in the resolution.

Article 24 *(contd.)*

2. ~~Where a Bill the time for the consideration of which by Seanad Éireann has been abridged under this Article is within the period specified in the resolution either rejected by Seanad Éireann or passed by Seanad Éireann with amendments or recommendations to which Dáil Éireann does not agree or is neither passed (with or without amendments or recommendations) nor rejected by Seanad Éireann within the period so specified the Bill shall be deemed to have been passed by both Houses of the Oireachtas at the expiration of that period.~~

2. Where a Bill, the time for the consideration of which by Seanad Éireann has been abridged under this Article,

   (a) is, in the case of a Bill which is not a Money Bill, rejected by Seanad Éireann or passed by Seanad Éireann with amendments to which Dáil Éireann does not agree or neither passed nor rejected by Seanad Éireann, or

   (b) is, in the case of a Money Bill, either returned by Seanad Éireann to Dáil Éireann with recommendations which Dáil Éireann does not accept or is not returned by Seanad Éireann to Dáil Éireann,

   within the period specified in the resolution, the Bill shall be deemed to have been passed by both Houses of the Oireachtas at the expiration of that period.[53]

3. When a Bill the time for the consideration of which by Seanad Éireann has been abridged under this Article becomes law it shall remain in force for a period of ninety days from the date of its enactment and no longer

---

53. Second Amendment of the Constitution Act, 1941, Ref. No. 9.

Article 24 *(contd.)*

unless, before the expiration of that period, both Houses shall have agreed that such law shall remain in force for a longer period and the longer period so agreed upon shall have been specified in resolutions passed by both Houses.

THE NATIONAL PARLIAMENT.

Legislation.

Signing and Promulgation of Laws.

Article 25.

1. As soon as any Bill, other than a Bill expressed to be a Bill containing a proposal for the amendment of this Constitution, shall have been passed or deemed to have been passed by both Houses of the Oireachtas, the Taoiseach shall present it to the President for his signature and for promulgation by him as a law in accordance with the provisions of this Article.

2. 1° Save as otherwise provided by this Constitution, every Bill so presented to the President for his signature and for promulgation by him as a law shall be signed by the President not earlier than ~~five~~ the fifth[54] and not later than ~~seven days~~ the seventh day[55]

---

54. Second Amendment of the Constitution Act, 1941, Ref. No. 10.
55. Second Amendment of the Constitution Act, 1941, Ref. No. 10.

Article 25 *(contd.)*

after the date on which the Bill shall have been presented to him.

2° At the request of the Government, with the prior concurrence of Seanad Éireann, the President may sign any Bill the subject of such request on a date which is earlier than ~~five days~~ the fifth day[56] after such date as aforesaid.

3. Every Bill the time for the consideration of which by Seanad Éireann shall have been abridged under Article 24 of this Constitution shall be signed by the President on the day on which such Bill is presented to him for signature and promulgation as a law.

4. 1° ~~Every Bill signed by the President under this Constitution shall become and be law as on and from the day on which the Bill shall have been so signed.~~

2° ~~Every Bill signed by the President shall come into operation of the day on which it is so signed unless the contrary intention appears.~~

3° ~~Every Bill so signed shall be promulgated by the President as a law by the publication by his direction of a notice in the Iris Oifigiúil stating that such Bill has become law.~~

4° ~~As soon as may be after the President has signed any Bill and promulgated it as a law, the signed text shall be enrolled for record in the office of the Registrar of the Supreme Court and such signed text shall be conclusive evidence as to the provisions of such law.~~

5° ~~An official translation of every law enacted by the~~

---

56. Second Amendment of the Constitution Act, 1941, Ref. No. 10.

Article 25 *(contd.)*

~~Oireachtas in the Irish language shall be issued in the English language and an official translation of every law enacted by the Oireachtas in the English language shall be issued in the Irish language.~~

4. 1°   Every Bill shall become and be law as on and from the day on which it is signed by the President under this Constitution, and shall, unless the contrary intention appears, come into operation on that day.

   2°   Every Bill signed by the President under this Constitution shall be promulgated by him as a law by the publication by his direction of a notice in the *Iris Oifigiúil* stating that the Bill has become law.

   3°   Every Bill shall be signed by the President in the text in which it was passed or deemed to have been passed by both Houses of the Oireachtas, and if a Bill is so passed or deemed to have been passed in both the official languages, the President shall sign the text of the Bill in each of those languages.

   4°   Where the President signs the text of a Bill in one only of the official languages, an official translation shall be issued in the other official language.

   5°   As soon as may be after the signature and promulgation of a Bill as a law, the text of such law which was signed by the President or where the President has signed the text of such law in each of the official languages, both the signed texts shall be enrolled for record in the office of the Registrar of the Supreme Court, and the text, or both the texts, so enrolled shall be conclusive evidence of the provisions of such law.

Article 25 *(contd.)*

6° In case of conflict between the texts of a law enrolled under this section in both the official languages, the text in the national language shall prevail.[57]

5. 1° It shall be lawful for the Taoiseach, from time to time as occasion appears to him to require, to cause to be prepared under his supervision a text (in both the official languages) of this Constitution as then in force embodying all amendments theretofore made therein.

2° A copy of every text so prepared, when authenticated by the signatures of the Taoiseach and the Chief Justice, shall be signed by the President and shall be enrolled for record in the office of the Registrar of the Supreme Court.

3° The copy so signed and enrolled which is for the time being the latest text so prepared shall, upon such enrolment, be conclusive evidence of this Constitution as at the date of such enrolment and shall for that purpose supersede all texts of this Constitution of which copies were previously so enrolled.

4° In case of conflict between the texts of any copy of this Constitution enrolled under this section, the text in the national language shall prevail.[58]

---

57. Second Amendment of the Constitution Act, 1941, Ref. No. 11.
58. Second Amendment of the Constitution Act, 1941, Ref. No. 12.

THE NATIONAL PARLIAMENT.

Legislation.

Reference of Bills to the Supreme Court.

Article 26.

This Article applies to any Bill passed or deemed to have been passed by both Houses of the Oireachtas other than a Money Bill, or a Bill expressed to be a Bill containing a proposal to amend the Constitution, or a Bill the time for the consideration of which by Seanad Éireann shall have been abridged under Article 24 of this Constitution.

1. 1° The President may, after consultation with the Council of State, refer any Bill to which this Article applies to the Supreme Court for a decision on the question as to whether such Bill or any specified provision or provisions of such Bill is or are repugnant to this Constitution or to any provision thereof.

Article 26 *(contd.)*

2° Every such reference shall be made not later than ~~four days~~ the seventh day[59] after the date on which such Bill shall have been ~~passed or deemed to have been passed by both Houses of the Oireachtas~~ presented by the Taoiseach to the President for his signature.[60]

3° The President shall not sign any Bill the subject of a reference to the Supreme Court under this Article pending the pronouncement of the decision of the Court.

2. 1° The Supreme Court consisting of not less than five judges shall consider every question referred to it by the President under this Article for a decision, and, having heard arguments by or on behalf of the Attorney General and by counsel assigned by the Court, shall pronounce its decision on such question in open court as soon as may be, and in any case not later than sixty days after the date of such reference.

2° The decision of the majority of the judges of the Supreme Court shall, for the purposes of this Article, be the decision of the Court and shall be pronounced by such one of those judges as the Court shall direct, and no other opinion, whether assenting or dissenting, shall be pronounced nor shall the existence of any such other opinion be disclosed.[61]

3. 1° In every case in which the Supreme Court decides that any provision of a Bill the subject of a reference to the Supreme Court under this Article is repugnant to this Constitution or to any provision thereof, the President shall decline to sign such Bill.

---

59. Second Amendment of the Constitution Act, 1941, Ref. No. 13.
60. Second Amendment of the Constitution Act, 1941, Ref. No. 14.
61. Second Amendment of the Constitution Act, 1941, Ref. No. 15.

Article 26 *(contd.)*

2° If, in the case of a Bill to which Article 27 of this Constitution applies, a petition has been addressed to the President under that Article, that Article shall be complied with.[62]

3° In every other case the President shall sign the Bill as soon as may be after the date on which the decision of the Supreme Court shall have been pronounced.

---

62. Second Amendment of the Constitution Act, 1941, Ref. No. 16.

THE NATIONAL PARLIAMENT.

Legislation.

Reference of Bills to the People.

Article 27.

This Article applies to any Bill, other than a Bill expressed to be a Bill containing a proposal for the amendment of this Constitution, which shall have been deemed, by virtue of Article 23 hereof, to have been passed by both Houses of the Oireachtas.

1. A majority of the members of Seanad Éireann and not less than one-third of the members of Dáil Éireann may by a joint petition addressed to the President by them under this Article request the President to decline to sign and promulgate as a law any Bill to which this Article applies on the ground that the Bill contains a proposal of such national importance that the will of the people thereon ought to be ascertained.

Article 27 *(contd.)*

2. Every such petition shall be in writing and shall be signed by the petitioners whose signatures shall be verified in the manner prescribed by law.[63]

~~2~~ 3. Every such petition ~~shall be in writing signed by the petitioners~~,[64] shall contain a statement of the particular ground or grounds on which the request is based, and shall be presented to the President not later than four days after the date on which the Bill shall have been deemed to have been passed by both Houses of the Oireachtas.

~~3~~ 4.1° Upon receipt of a petition addressed to him under this Article, the President shall forthwith consider such petition and shall, after consultation with the Council of State, pronounce his decision thereon not later than ten days after the date on which the Bill to which such petition relates shall have been deemed to have been passed by both Houses of the Oireachtas.

2° If the Bill or any provision thereof is or has been referred to the Supreme Court under Article 26 of this Constitution, it shall not be obligatory on the President to consider the petition unless or until the Supreme Court has pronounced a decision on such reference to the effect that the said Bill or the said provision thereof is not repugnant to this Constitution or to any provision thereof, and, if a decision to that effect is pronounced by the Supreme Court, it shall not be obligatory on the President to pronounce his decision on the petition before the expiration of six days after the day on which the decision of the Supreme Court to the effect aforesaid is pronounced.[65]

---

63. Second Amendment of the Constitution Act, 1941, Ref. No. 17.
64. Second Amendment of the Constitution Act, 1941, Ref. No. 17.
65. Second Amendment of the Constitution Act, 1941, Ref. No. 18.

Article 27 *(contd.)*

4 **5**.1° In every case in which the President decides that a Bill the subject of a petition under this Article contains a proposal of such national importance that the will of the people thereon ought to be ascertained, he shall inform the Taoiseach and the Chairman of each House of the Oireachtas accordingly in writing under his hand and Seal and shall decline to sign and promulgate such Bill as a law unless and until the proposal shall have been approved either

   i.   by the people at a Referendum in accordance with the provisions of section 2 of Article 47 of this Constitution within a period of eighteen months from the date of the President's decision, or

   ii. by a resolution of Dáil Éireann passed within the said period after a dissolution and re-assembly of Dáil Éireann.

   2° ~~Every such Bill which~~ Whenever a proposal contained in a Bill the subject of a petition under this Article[66] shall have been approved either by the people or by a resolution of Dáil Éireann in accordance with the foregoing provisions of this section, such Bill[67] shall as soon as may be after such approval be presented to the President for his signature and promulgation by him as a law and the President shall thereupon sign the Bill and duly promulgate it as a law.

5 **6**.   In every case in which the President decides that a Bill the subject of a petition under this Article does not contain a proposal of such national importance

---

66. Second Amendment of the Constitution Act, 1941, Ref. No. 19.
67. Second Amendment of the Constitution Act, 1941, Ref. No. 19.

Article 27 *(contd.)*

that the will of the people thereon ought to be ascertained, he shall inform the Taoiseach and the Chairman of each House of the Oireachtas accordingly in writing under his hand and Seal, and such Bill shall be signed by the President not later than eleven days after the date on which the Bill shall have been deemed to have been passed by both Houses of the Oireachtas and shall be duly promulgated by him as a law.

THE GOVERNMENT.

Article 28.

1. The Government shall consist of not less than seven and not more than fifteen members who shall be appointed by the President in accordance with the provisions of this Constitution.

2. The executive power of the State shall, subject to the provisions of this Constitution, be exercised by or on the authority of the Government.

3. 1° War shall not be declared and the State shall not participate in any war save with the assent of Dáil Éireann.

Article 28 *(contd.)*

2° In the case of actual invasion, however, the Government may take whatever steps they may consider necessary for the protection of the State, and Dáil Éireann if not sitting shall be summoned to meet at the earliest practicable date.

3° Nothing in this Constitution shall be invoked to invalidate any law enacted by the Oireachtas which is expressed to be for the purpose of securing the public safety and the preservation of the State in time of war or armed rebellion, or to nullify any act done or purporting to be done in time of war or armed rebellion[68] in pursuance of any such law. In this subsection 'time of war' includes a time when there is taking place an armed conflict in which the State is not a participant but in respect of which each of the Houses of the Oireachtas shall have resolved that, arising out of such armed conflict, a national emergency exists affecting the vital interests of the State[69] and 'time of war or armed rebellion' includes such time after the termination of any war, or of any such armed conflict as aforesaid, or of an armed rebellion, as may elapse until each of the Houses of the Oireachtas shall have resolved that the national emergency occasioned by such war, armed conflict, or armed rebellion has ceased to exist.[70]

4. 1° The Government shall be responsible to Dáil Éireann.

2° The Government shall meet and act as a collective authority, and shall be collectively responsible for the Departments of State administered by the members of the Government.

68. Second Amendment of the Constitution Act, 1941, Ref. No. 20.
69. First Amendment of the Constitution Act, 1939.
70. Second Amendment of the Constitution Act, 1941, Ref. No. 22.

Article 28 *(contd.)*

3° The Government shall prepare Estimates of the Receipts and Estimates of the Expenditure of the State for each financial year, and shall present them to Dáil Éireann for consideration.

5. 1° The head of the Government, or Prime Minister, shall be called, and is in this Constitution referred to as, the Taoiseach.

2° The Taoiseach shall keep the President generally informed on matters of domestic and international policy.

6. 1° The Taoiseach shall nominate a member of the Government to be the Tánaiste.

2° The Tánaiste shall act for all purposes in the place of the Taoiseach if the Taoiseach should die, or become permanently incapacitated, until a new Taoiseach shall have been appointed.

3° The Tánaiste shall also act for or in the place of the Taoiseach during the temporary absence of the Taoiseach.

7. 1° The Taoiseach, the Tánaiste and the member of the Government who is in charge of the Department of Finance must be members of Dáil Éireann.

2° The other members of the Government must be members of Dáil Éireann or Seanad Éireann, but not more than two may be members of Seanad Éireann.

8. Every member of the Government shall have the right to attend and be heard in each House of the Oireachtas.

Article 28 *(contd.)*

9. 1° The Taoiseach may resign from office at any time by placing his resignation in the hands of the President.

    2° Any other member of the Government may resign from office by placing his resignation in the hands of the Taoiseach for submission to the President.

    3° The President shall accept the resignation of a member of the Government, other than the Taoiseach, if so advised by the Taoiseach.

    4° The Taoiseach may at any time, for reasons which to him seem sufficient, request a member of the Government to resign; should the member concerned fail to comply with the request, his appointment shall be terminated by the President if the Taoiseach so advises.

10. The Taoiseach shall resign from office upon his ceasing to retain the support of a majority in Dáil Éireann unless on his advice the President dissolves Dáil Éireann and on the reassembly of Dáil Éireann after the dissolution the Taoiseach secures the support of a majority in Dáil Éireann.

11. 1° If the Taoiseach at any time resigns from office the other members of the Government shall be deemed also to have resigned from office, but the Taoiseach and the other members of the Government shall continue to carry on their duties until their successors shall have been appointed.

    2° The members of the Government in office at the date of a dissolution of Dáil Éireann shall continue to hold office until their successors shall have been appointed.

Article 28 *(contd.)*

12. The following matters shall be regulated in accordance
    with law, namely, the organization of, and distribution
    of business amongst, Departments of State, the
    designation of members of the Government to be the
    Ministers in charge of the said Departments, the
    discharge of the functions of the office of a member of
    the Government during his temporary absence or
    incapacity, and the remuneration of the members of the
    Government.

INTERNATIONAL RELATIONS.

Article 29.

1. Ireland affirms its devotion to the ideal of peace and friendly co-operation amongst nations founded on international justice and morality.

2. Ireland affirms its adherence to the principle of pacific settlement of international disputes by international arbitration or judicial determination.

3. Ireland accepts the generally recognised principles of international law as its rule of conduct in its relations with other States.

4. 1° The executive power of the State in or in connection with its external relations shall in accordance with Article 28 of this Constitution be exercised by or on the authority of the Government.

Article 29 *(contd.)*

2° For the purpose of the exercise of any executive function of the State in or in connection with its external relations, the Government may to such extent and subject to such conditions, if any, as may be determined by law, avail of or adopt any organ, instrument, or method of procedure used or adopted for the like purpose by the members of any group or league of nations with which the State is or becomes associated for the purpose of international co-operation in matters of common concern.

3° The State may become a member of the European Coal and Steel Community (established by Treaty signed at Paris on the 18th day of April, 1951), the European Economic Community (established by Treaty signed at Rome on the 25th day of March, 1957) and the European Atomic Energy Community (established by Treaty signed at Rome on the 25th day of March, 1957).[71] The State may ratify the Single European Act (signed on behalf of the Member States of the Communities at Luxembourg on the 17th day of February, 1986, and at The Hague on the 28th day of February, 1986).[72] ~~No provision of this Constitution invalidates laws enacted, acts done or measures adopted by the State necessitated by the obligations of membership of the Communities or prevents laws enacted, acts done or measures adopted by the Communities, or institutions thereof, from having the force of law in the State.~~[73]

---

71. Third Amendment of the Constitution Act, 1972.
72. Tenth Amendment of the Constitution Act, 1987.
73. Text added by the Third Amendment of the Constitution Act, 1972, but a portion was struck out by the Eleventh Amendment of the Constitution Act, 1992.

Article 29 *(contd.)*

4° The State may ratify the Treaty on European Union signed at Maastricht on the 7th day of February, 1992, and may become a member of that Union.

5° No provision of this Constitution invalidates laws enacted, acts done or measures adopted by the State which are necessitated by the obligations of membership of the European Union or of the Communities, or prevents laws enacted, acts done or measures adopted by the European Union or by the Communities or by institutions thereof, or by bodies competent under the Treaties establishing the Communities, from having the force of law in the State.

6° The State may ratify the Agreement relating to Community Patents drawn up between the Member States of the Communities and done at Luxembourg on the 15th day of December, 1989.[74]

5. 1° Every international agreement to which the State becomes a party shall be laid before Dáil Éireann.

2° The State shall not be bound by any international agreement involving a charge upon public funds unless the terms of the agreement shall have been approved by Dáil Éireann.

3° This section shall not apply to agreements or conventions of a technical and administrative character.

---

74. Eleventh Amendment of the Constitution Act, 1992.

Article 29 *(contd.)*

6. No international agreement shall be part of the domestic
    law of the State save as may be determined by the
    Oireachtas.

THE ATTORNEY GENERAL.

Article 30.

1. There shall be an Attorney General who shall be the adviser of the Government in matters of law and legal opinion, and shall exercise and perform all such powers, functions and duties as are conferred or imposed on him by this Constitution or by law.

2. The Attorney General shall be appointed by the President on the nomination of the Taoiseach.

3. All crimes and offences prosecuted in any court constituted under Article 34 of this Constitution other than a court of summary jurisdiction shall be prosecuted in the name of the People and at the suit of the Attorney General or some other person authorised in accordance with law to act for that purpose.

Article 30 *(contd.)*

4. The Attorney General shall not be a member of the Government.

5. 1° The Attorney General may at any time resign from office by placing his resignation in the hands of the Taoiseach for submission to the President.

   2° The Taoiseach may, for reasons which to him seem sufficient, request the resignation of the Attorney General.

   3° In the event of failure to comply with the request, the appointment of the Attorney General shall be terminated by the President if the Taoiseach so advises.

   4° The Attorney General shall retire from office upon the resignation of the Taoiseach, but may continue to carry on his duties until the successor to the Taoiseach shall have been appointed.

6. Subject to the foregoing provisions of this Article, the office of Attorney General, including the remuneration to be paid to the holder of the office, shall be regulated by law.

THE COUNCIL OF STATE.

Article 31.

1. There shall be a Council of State to aid and counsel the President on all matters on which the President may consult the said Council in relation to the exercise and performance by him of such of his powers and functions as are by this Constitution expressed to be exercisable and performable after consultation with the Council of State, and to exercise such other functions as are conferred on the said Council by this Constitution.

2. The Council of State shall consist of the following members:

   i.   As *ex-officio* members: the Taoiseach, the Tánaiste, the Chief Justice, the President of the High Court, the Chairman of Dáil Éireann, the Chairman of Seanad Éireann, and the Attorney General.

Article 31 *(contd.)*

    ii. Every person able and willing to act as a member of the Council of State who shall have held the office of President, or the office of Taoiseach, or the office of Chief Justice, or the office of President of the Executive Council of Saorstát Éireann.

    iii. Such other persons, if any, as may be appointed by the President under this Article to be members of the Council of State.

3. The President may at any time and from time to time by warrant under his hand and Seal appoint such other persons as, in his absolute discretion, he may think fit, to be members of the Council of State, but not more than seven persons so appointed shall be members of the Council of State at the same time.

4. Every member of the Council of State shall at the first meeting thereof which he attends as a member take and subscribe a declaration in the following form:

> "In the presence of Almighty God I
> do solemnly and sincerely promise and declare that
> I will faithfully and conscientiously fulfil my duties
> as a member of the Council of State."

5. Every member of the Council of State appointed by the President, unless he previously dies, resigns, becomes permanently incapacitated, or is removed from office, shall hold office until the successor of the President by whom he was appointed shall have entered upon his office.

6. Any member of the Council of State appointed by the President may resign from office by placing his resignation in the hands of the President.

Article 31 *(contd.)*

7. The President may, for reasons which to him seem sufficient, by an order under his hand and Seal, terminate the appointment of any member of the Council of State appointed by him.

8. Meetings of the Council of State may be convened by the President at such times and places as he shall determine.

THE COUNCIL OF STATE.

Article 32.

The President shall not exercise or perform any of the powers or functions which are by this Constitution expressed to be exercisable or performable by him after consultation with the Council of State unless, and on every occasion before so doing, he shall have convened a meeting of the Council of State and the members present at such meeting shall have been heard by him.

THE COMPTROLLER AND AUDITOR GENERAL.

Article 33.

1. There shall be a Comptroller and Auditor General to control on behalf of the State all disbursements and to audit all accounts of moneys administered by or under the authority of the Oireachtas.

2. The Comptroller and Auditor General shall be appointed by the President on the nomination of Dáil Éireann.

3. The Comptroller and Auditor General shall not be a member of either House of the Oireachtas and shall not hold any other office or position of emolument.

4. The Comptroller and Auditor General shall report to Dáil Éireann at stated periods as determined by law.

Article 33 *(contd.)*

5. 1° The Comptroller and Auditor General shall not be removed from office except for stated misbehaviour or incapacity, and then only upon resolutions passed by Dáil Éireann and by Seanad Éireann calling for his removal.

 2° The Taoiseach shall duly notify the President of any such resolutions as aforesaid passed by Dáil Éireann and by Seanad Éireann and shall send him a copy of each such resolution certified by the Chairman of the House of the Oireachtas by which it shall have been passed.

 3° Upon receipt of such notification and of copies of such resolutions, the President shall forthwith, by an order under his hand and Seal, remove the Comptroller and Auditor General from office.

6. Subject to the foregoing, the terms and conditions of the office of Comptroller and Auditor General shall be determined by law.

THE COURTS.

Article 34.

1. ~~Justice shall be administered in public courts established by law by judges appointed in the manner provided by this Constitution.~~

1. Justice shall be administered in courts established by law by judges appointed in the manner provided by this Constitution, and, save in such special and limited cases as may be prescribed by law, shall be administered in public.[75]

2. The Courts shall comprise Courts of First Instance and a Court of Final Appeal.

---

75. Second Amendment of the Constitution Act, 1941, Ref. No. 23.

Article 34 *(contd.)*

3. 1° The Courts of First Instance shall include a High Court invested with full original jurisdiction in and power to determine all matters and questions whether of law or fact, civil or criminal.

   2° ~~The jurisdiction of the High Court shall extend to the question of the validity of any law having regard to the provisions of this Constitution, and in all cases in which any such matter shall come into question the High Court alone shall exercise original jurisdiction.~~[76]

   2° Save as otherwise provided by this Article, the jurisdiction of the High Court shall extend to the question of the validity of any law having regard to the provisions of this Constitution, and no such question shall be raised (whether by pleading, argument or otherwise) in any Court established under this or any other Article of this Constitution other than the High Court or the Supreme Court.

   3° No Court whatever shall have jurisdiction to question the validity of a law, or any provision of a law, the Bill for which shall have been referred to the Supreme Court by the President under Article 26 of this Constitution, or to question the validity of a provision of a law where the corresponding provision in the Bill for such law shall have been referred to the Supreme Court by the President under the said Article 26.[77]

   4° The Courts of First Instance shall also include Courts of local and limited jurisdiction with a right of appeal as determined by law.

---

76. Second Amendment of the Constitution Act, 1941, Ref. No. 24.
77. Second Amendment of the Constitution Act, 1941, Ref. No. 24.

Article 34 *(contd.)*

4. 1° The Court of Final Appeal shall be called the Supreme Court.

   2° The president of the Supreme Court shall be called the Chief Justice.

   3° The Supreme Court shall, with such exceptions and subject to such regulations as may be prescribed by law, have appellate jurisdiction from all decisions of the High Court, and shall also have appellate jurisdiction from such decisions of other courts as may be prescribed by law.

   4° No law shall be enacted excepting from the appellate jurisdiction of the Supreme Court cases which involve questions as to the validity of any law having regard to the provisions of this Constitution.

   5° The decision of the Supreme Court on a question as to the validity of a law having regard to the provisions of this Constitution shall be pronounced by such one of the judges of that Court as that Court shall direct, and no other opinion on such question, whether assenting or dissenting, shall be pronounced, nor shall the existence of any such other opinion be disclosed.[78]

   6° The decision of the Supreme Court shall in all cases be final and conclusive.

5. 1° Every person appointed a judge under this Constitution shall make and subscribe the following declaration:

---

78. Second Amendment of the Constitution Act, 1941, Ref. No. 25.

Article 34 *(contd.)*

> "In the presence of Almighty God I,
> do solemnly and sincerely promise and declare
> that I will duly and faithfully and to the best of
> my knowledge and power execute the office of
> Chief Justice *(or as the case may be)* without
> fear or favour, affection or ill-will towards any
> man, and that I will uphold the Constitution and
> the laws. May God direct and sustain me."

2° This declaration shall be made and subscribed by the Chief Justice in the presence of the President, and by each of the other judges of the Supreme Court, the judges of the High Court and the judges of every other Court in the presence of the Chief Justice or the senior available judge of the Supreme Court in open court.

3° The declaration shall be made and subscribed by every judge before entering upon his duties as such judge, and in any case not later than ten days after the date of his appointment or such later date as may be determined by the President.

4° Any judge who declines or neglects to make such declaration as aforesaid shall be deemed to have vacated his office.

THE COURTS.

Article 35.

1. The judges of the Supreme Court, the High Court and all other Courts established in pursuance of Article 34 hereof shall be appointed by the President.

2. All judges shall be independent in the exercise of their judicial functions and subject only to this Constitution and the law.

3. No judge shall be eligible to be a member of either House of the Oireachtas or to hold any other office or position of emolument.

Article 35 *(contd.)*

4. 1° A judge of the Supreme Court or the High Court shall not be removed from office except for stated misbehaviour or incapacity, and then only upon resolutions passed by Dáil Éireann and by Seanad Éireann calling for his removal.

    2° The Taoiseach shall duly notify the President of any such resolutions passed by Dáil Éireann and by Seanad Éireann, and shall send him a copy of every such resolution certified by the Chairman of the House of the Oireachtas by which it shall have been passed.

    3° Upon receipt of such notification and of copies of such resolutions, the President shall forthwith, by an order under his hand and Seal, remove from office the judge to whom they relate.

5. The remuneration of a judge shall not be reduced during his continuance in office.

THE COURTS.

Article 36.

Subject to the foregoing provisions of this Constitution relating to the Courts, the following matters shall be regulated in accordance with law, that is to say:—

i. the number of judges of the Supreme Court, and of the High Court, the remuneration, age of retirement and pensions of such judges,

ii. the number of the judges of all other Courts, and their terms of appointment, and

iii. the constitution and organization of the said Courts, the distribution of jurisdiction and business among the said Courts and judges, and all matters of procedure.

THE COURTS.

Article 37.

1. Nothing in this Constitution shall operate to invalidate the exercise of limited functions and powers of a judicial nature, in matters other than criminal matters, by any person or body of persons duly authorised by law to exercise such functions and powers, notwithstanding that such person or such body of persons is not a judge or a court appointed or established as such under this Constitution.

2. No adoption of a person taking effect or expressed to take effect at any time after the coming into operation of this Constitution under laws enacted by the Oireachtas and being an adoption pursuant to an order made or an authorisation given by any person or

Article 37 *(contd.)*

body of persons designated by those laws to exercise such functions and powers was or shall be invalid by reason only of the fact that such persons or body of persons was not a judge or a court appointed or established as such under this Constitution.[79]

79. Sixth Amendment of the Constitution Act, 1979.

TRIAL OF OFFENCES.

Article 38.

1. No person shall be tried on any criminal charge save in due course of law.

2. Minor offences may be tried by courts of summary jurisdiction.

3. 1° Special courts may be established by law for the trial of offences in cases where it may be determined in accordance with such law that the ordinary courts are inadequate to secure the effective administration of justice, and the preservation of public peace and order.

Article 38 *(contd.)*

2° The constitution, powers, jurisdiction and procedure of such special courts shall be prescribed by law.

4. 1° Military tribunals may be established for the trial of offences against military law alleged to have been committed by persons while subject to military law and also to deal with a state of war or armed rebellion.

   2° A member of the Defence Forces not on active service shall not be tried by any courtmartial or other military tribunal for an offence cognisable by the civil courts unless such offence is within the jurisdiction of any courtmartial or other military tribunal under any law for the enforcement of military discipline.

5. Save in the case of trial of offences under section 2, section 3 or section 4 of this Article no person shall be tried on any criminal charge without a jury.

6. The provisions of Articles 34 and 35 of this Constitution shall not apply to any court or tribunal set up under section 3 or section 4 of this Article.

TRIAL OF OFFENCES.

Article 39.

Treason shall consist only in levying war against the State, or assisting any State or person or inciting or conspiring with any person to levy war against the State, or attempting by force of arms or other violent means to overthrow the organs of government established by this Constitution, or taking part or being concerned in or inciting or conspiring with any person to make or to take part or be concerned in any such attempt.

FUNDAMENTAL RIGHTS.

Personal Rights.

Article 40.

1. All citizens shall, as human persons, be held equal before the law. This shall not be held to mean that the State shall not in its enactments have due regard to differences of capacity, physical and moral, and of social function.

2. 1° Titles of nobility shall not be conferred by the State.

   2° No title of nobility or of honour may be accepted by any citizen except with the prior approval of the Government.

3. 1° The State guarantees in its laws to respect, and, as far as practicable, by its laws to defend and vindicate the personal rights of the citizen.

Article 40 *(contd.)*

2° The State shall, in particular, by its laws protect as best it may from unjust attack and, in the case of injustice done, vindicate the life, person, good name, and property rights of every citizen.

3° The State acknowledges the right to life of the unborn and, with due regard to the equal right to life of the mother, guarantees in its laws to respect, and, as far as practicable, by its laws to defend and vindicate that right.[80]

This subsection shall not limit freedom to travel between the State and another state.[81]

This subsection shall not limit freedom to obtain or make available, in the State, subject to such conditions as may be laid down by law, information relating to services lawfully available in another state.[82]

4. 1° No citizen shall be deprived of his personal liberty save in accordance with law.

2° ~~Upon complaint being made by or on behalf of any person that he is being unlawfully detained, the High Court and any and every judge thereof shall forthwith enquire into the same and may make an order requiring the person in whose custody such person shall be detained to produce the body of the person so detained before such court or judge without delay and to certify in writing as to the cause of the detention, and such Court or judge shall thereupon order the release of such person unless satisfied that he is being detained in accordance with the law.~~[83]

---

80. Eighth Amendment of the Constitution Act, 1983.
81. Thirteenth Amendment of the Constitution Act, 1992.
82. Fourteenth Amendment of the Constitution Act, 1992.
83. Second Amendment of the Constitution Act, 1941, Ref. No. 27.

Article 40 *(contd.)*

2°   Upon complaint being made by or on behalf of any person to the High Court or any judge thereof alleging that such person is being unlawfully detained, the High Court and any and every judge thereof to whom such complaint is made shall forthwith enquire into the said complaint and may order the person in whose custody such person is detained to produce the body of such person before the High Court on a named day and to certify in writing the grounds of his detention, and the High Court shall, upon the body of such person being produced before that Court and after giving the person in whose custody he is detained an opportunity of justifying the detention, order the release of such person from such detention unless satisfied that he is being detained in accordance with the law.[84]

3°   Where the body of a person alleged to be unlawfully detained is produced before the High Court in pursuance of an order in that behalf made under this section and that Court is satisfied that such person is being detained in accordance with a law but that such law is invalid having regard to the provisions of this Constitution, the High Court shall refer the question of the validity of such law to the Supreme Court by way of case stated and may, at the time of such reference or at any time thereafter, allow the said person to be at liberty on such bail and subject to such conditions as the High Court shall fix until the Supreme Court has determined the question so referred to it.[85]

---

84. Second Amendment of the Constitution Act, 1941, Ref. No. 27.
85. Second Amendment of the Constitution Act, 1941, Ref. No. 27.

Article 40 *(contd.)*

4° The High Court before which the body of a person alleged to be unlawfully detained is to be produced in pursuance of an order in that behalf made under this section shall, if the President of the High Court or, if he is not available, the senior judge of that Court who is available so directs in respect of any particular case, consist of three judges and shall, in every other case, consist of one judge only.[86]

5° Where an order is made under this section by the High Court or a judge thereof for the production of the body of a person who is under sentence of death, the High Court or such judge thereof shall further order that the execution of the said sentence of death shall be deferred until after the body of such person has been produced before the High Court and the lawfulness of his detention has been determined and if, after such deferment, the detention of such person is determined to be lawful, the High Court shall appoint a day for the execution of the said sentence of death and that sentence shall have effect with the substitution of the day so appointed for the day originally fixed for the execution thereof.[87]

6° Nothing in this section, however, shall be invoked to prohibit, control, or interfere with any act of the Defence Forces during the existence of a state of war or armed rebellion.

5. The dwelling of every citizen is inviolable and shall not be forcibly entered save in accordance with law.

---

86. Second Amendment of the Constitution Act, 1941, Ref. No. 27.
87. Second Amendment of the Constitution Act, 1941, Ref. No. 27.

Article 40 *(contd.)*

6. 1° The State guarantees liberty for the exercise of the following rights, subject to public order and morality:—

    i. The right of the citizens to express freely their convictions and opinions.

        The education of public opinion being, however, a matter of such grave import to the common good, the State shall endeavour to ensure that organs of public opinion, such as the radio, the press, the cinema, while preserving their rightful liberty of expression, including criticism of Government policy, shall not be used to undermine public order or morality or the authority of the State.

        The publication or utterance of blasphemous, seditious, or indecent matter is an offence which shall be punishable in accordance with law.

    ii. The right of the citizens to assemble peaceably and without arms.

        Provision may be made by law to prevent or control meetings which are determined in accordance with law to be calculated to cause a breach of the peace or to be a danger or nuisance to the general public and to prevent or control meetings in the vicinity of either House of the Oireachtas.

    iii. The right of the citizens to form associations and unions.

Article 40 *(contd.)*

> Laws, however, may be enacted for the regulation and control in the public interest of the exercise of the foregoing right.

2° Laws regulating the manner in which the right of forming associations and unions and the right of free assembly may be exercised shall contain no political, religious or class discrimination.

FUNDAMENTAL RIGHTS.

The Family.

Article 41.

1. 1° The State recognises the Family as the natural primary and fundamental unit group of Society, and as a moral institution possessing inalienable and imprescriptible rights, antecedent and superior to all positive law.

   2° The State, therefore, guarantees to protect the Family in its constitution and authority, as the necessary basis of social order and as indispensable to the welfare of the Nation and the State.

2. 1° In particular, the State recognises that by her life within the home, woman gives to the State a support without which the common good cannot be achieved.

Article 41 *(contd.)*

2° The State shall, therefore, endeavour to ensure that mothers shall not be obliged by economic necessity to engage in labour to the neglect of their duties in the home.

3. 1° The State pledges itself to guard with special care the institution of Marriage, on which the Family is founded, and to protect it against attack.

2° No law shall be enacted providing for the grant of a dissolution of marriage.

3° No person whose marriage has been dissolved under the civil law of any other State but is a subsisting valid marriage under the law for the time being in force within the jurisdiction of the Government and Parliament established by this Constitution shall be capable of contracting a valid marriage within that jurisdiction during the lifetime of the other party to the marriage so dissolved.

FUNDAMENTAL RIGHTS.

Education.

Article 42.

1. The State acknowledges that the primary and natural educator of the child is the Family and guarantees to respect the inalienable right and duty of parents to provide, according to their means, for the religious and moral, intellectual, physical and social education of their children.

2. Parents shall be free to provide this education in their homes or in private schools or in schools recognised or established by the State.

3. 1° The State shall not oblige parents in violation of their conscience and lawful preference to send their children to schools established by the State, or to any particular type of school designated by the State.

Article 42 *(contd.)*

2° The State shall, however, as guardian of the common good, require in view of actual conditions that the children receive a certain minimum education, moral, intellectual and social.

4. The State shall provide for free primary education and shall endeavour to supplement and give reasonable aid to private and corporate educational initiative, and, when the public good requires it, provide other educational facilities or institutions with due regard, however, for the rights of parents, especially in the matter of religious and moral formation.

5. In exceptional cases, where the parents for physical or moral reasons fail in their duty towards their children, the State as guardian of the common good, by appropriate means shall endeavour to supply the place of the parents, but always with due regard for the natural and imprescriptible rights of the child.

FUNDAMENTAL RIGHTS.

Private Property.

Article 43.

1. 1° The State acknowledges that man, in virtue of his rational being, has the natural right, antecedent to positive law, to the private ownership of external goods.

   2° The State accordingly guarantees to pass no law attempting to abolish the right of private ownership or the general right to transfer, bequeath, and inherit property.

2. 1° The State recognises, however, that the exercise of the rights mentioned in the foregoing provisions of this Article ought, in civil society, to be regulated by the principles of social justice.

Article 43 *(contd.)*

2° The State, accordingly, may as occasion requires delimit by law the exercise of the said rights with a view to reconciling their exercise with the exigencies of the common good.

FUNDAMENTAL RIGHTS.

Religion.

Article 44.

1. The State acknowledges that the homage of public worship is due to Almighty God. It shall hold His Name in reverence, and shall respect and honour religion.

   2° ~~The State recognises the special position of the Holy Catholic Apostolic and Roman Church as the guardian of the Faith professed by the great majority of the citizens.~~

   3° ~~The State also recognises the Church of Ireland, the Presbyterian Church in Ireland, the Methodist Church in Ireland, the Religious Society of Friends in Ireland, as well as the Jewish Congregations and the other religious~~

Article 44 *(contd.)*

~~denominations existing in Ireland at the date of the coming into operation of this Constitution.~~[88]

2. 1° Freedom of conscience and the free profession and practice of religion are, subject to public order and morality, guaranteed to every citizen.

   2° The State guarantees not to endow any religion.

   3° The State shall not impose any disabilities or make any discrimination on the ground of religious profession, belief or status.

   4° Legislation providing State aid for schools shall not discriminate between schools under the management of different religious denominations, nor be such as to affect prejudicially the right of any child to attend a school receiving public money without attending religious instruction at that school.

   5° Every religious denomination shall have the right to manage its own affairs, own, acquire and administer property, movable and immovable, and maintain institutions for religious or charitable purposes.

   6° The property of any religious denomination or any educational institution shall not be diverted save for necessary works of public utility and on payment of compensation.

---

88. Fifth Amendment of the Constitution Act, 1972.

DIRECTIVE PRINCIPLES OF SOCIAL POLICY.

Article 45.

The principles of social policy set forth in this Article are intended for the general guidance of the Oireachtas. The application of those principles in the making of laws shall be the care of the Oireachtas exclusively, and shall not be cognisable by any Court under any of the provisions of this Constitution.

1. The State shall strive to promote the welfare of the whole people by securing and protecting as effectively as it may a social order in which justice and charity shall inform all the institutions of the national life.

2. The State shall, in particular, direct its policy towards securing:—

Article 45 *(contd.)*

i. That the citizens (all of whom, men and women equally, have the right to an adequate means of livelihood) may through their occupations find the means of making reasonable provision for their domestic needs.

ii. That the ownership and control of the material resources of the community may be so distributed amongst private individuals and the various classes as best to subserve the common good.

iii. That, especially, the operation of free competition shall not be allowed so to develop as to result in the concentration of the ownership or control of essential commodities in a few individuals to the common detriment.

iv. That in what pertains to the control of credit the constant and predominant aim shall be the welfare of the people as a whole.

v. That there may be established on the land in economic security as many families as in the circumstances shall be practicable.

3. 1° The State shall favour and, where necessary, supplement private initiative in industry and commerce.

    2° The State shall endeavour to secure that private enterprise shall be so conducted as to ensure reasonable efficiency in the production and distribution of goods and as to protect the public against unjust exploitation.

Article 45 *(contd.)*

4. 1° The State pledges itself to safeguard with especial care the economic interests of the weaker sections of the community, and, where necessary, to contribute to the support of the infirm, the widow, the orphan, and the aged.

    2° The State shall endeavour to ensure that the strength and health of workers, men and women, and the tender age of children shall not be abused and that citizens shall not be forced by economic necessity to enter avocations unsuited to their sex, age or strength.

AMENDMENT OF THE CONSTITUTION.

Article 46.

1. Any provision of this Constitution may be amended, whether by way of variation, addition, or repeal, in the manner provided by this Article.

2. Every proposal for an amendment of this Constitution shall be initiated in Dáil Éireann as a Bill, and shall upon having been passed or deemed to have been passed by both Houses of the Oireachtas, be submitted by Referendum to the decision of the people in accordance with the law for the time being in force relating to the Referendum.

3. Every such Bill shall be expressed to be "An Act to amend the Constitution".

Article 46 *(contd.)*

4. A Bill containing a proposal or proposals for the amendment of this Constitution shall not contain any other proposal.

5. A Bill containing a proposal for the amendment of this Constitution shall be signed by the President forthwith upon his being satisfied that the provisions of this Article have been complied with in respect thereof and that such proposal has been duly approved by the people in accordance with the provisions of section 1 of Article 47 of this Constitution and shall be duly promulgated by the President as a law.

THE REFERENDUM.

Article 47.

1. Every proposal for an amendment of this Constitution which is submitted by Referendum to the decision of the people shall, for the purpose of Article 46 of this Constitution, be held to have been approved by the people, if, upon having been so submitted, a majority of the votes cast at such Referendum shall have been cast in favour of its enactment into law.

2. 1° ~~Every Bill and~~[89] Every proposal, other than a proposal to amend the Constitution, which is submitted by Referendum to the decision of the people shall be held to have been vetoed by the people if a majority

---

89. Second Amendment of the Constitution Act, 1941, Ref. No. 28.

Article 47 *(contd.)*

of the votes cast at such Referendum shall have been cast against its enactment into law and if the votes so cast against its enactment into law shall have amounted to not less than thirty-three and one-third per cent. of the voters on the register.

2°   ~~Every Bill and~~[90] Every proposal, other than a proposal to amend the Constitution, which is submitted by Referendum to the decision of the people shall for the purposes of Article 27 hereof be held to have been approved by the people unless vetoed by them in accordance with the provision of the foregoing sub-section of this section.

3.   Every citizen who has the right to vote at an election for members of Dáil Éireann shall have the right to vote at a Referendum.

4.   Subject as aforesaid, the Referendum shall be regulated by law.

---

90. Second Amendment of the Constitution Act, 1941, Ref. No. 28.

REPEAL OF CONSTITUTION OF SAORSTÁT ÉIREANN AND CONTINUANCE OF LAWS.

Article 48.

The Constitution of Saorstát Éireann in force immediately prior to the date of the coming into operation of this Constitution and the Constitution of the Irish Free State (Saorstát Éireann) Act, 1922, in so far as that Act or any provision thereof is then in force shall be and are hereby repealed as on and from that date.

REPEAL OF CONSTITUTION OF SAORSTÁT ÉIREANN AND CONTINUANCE OF LAWS.

Article 49.

1. All powers, functions, rights and prerogatives whatsoever exercisable in or in respect of Saorstát Éireann immediately before the 11th day of December, 1936, whether in virtue of the Constitution then in force or otherwise, by the authority in which the executive power of Saorstát Éireann was then vested are hereby declared to belong to the people.

2. It is hereby enacted that, save to the extent to which provision is made by this Constitution or may hereafter be made by law for the exercise of any such power, function, right or prerogative by any of the organs established by this Constitution, the said powers,

Article 49 *(contd.)*

functions, rights and prerogatives shall not be exercised or be capable of being exercised in or in respect of the State save only by or on the authority of the Government.

3. The Government shall be the successors of the Government of Saorstát Éireann as regards all property, assets, rights and liabilities.

REPEAL OF CONSTITUTION OF SAORSTÁT ÉIREANN AND CONTINUANCE OF LAWS.

Article 50.

1. Subject to this Constitution and to the extent to which they are not inconsistent therewith, the laws in force in Saorstát Éireann immediately prior to the date of the coming into operation of this Constitution shall continue to be of full force and effect until the same or any of them shall have been repealed or amended by enactment of the Oireachtas.

2. Laws enacted before, but expressed to come into force after, the coming into operation of this Constitution, shall, unless otherwise enacted by the Oireachtas, come into force in accordance with the terms thereof.

TRANSITORY PROVISIONS.

Article 51.

1. Notwithstanding anything contained in Article 46 hereof, any of the provisions of this Constitution, except the provisions of the said Article 46 and this Article, may, subject as hereinafter provided, be amended by the Oireachtas, whether by way of variation, addition or repeal, within a period of three years after the date on which the first President shall have entered upon his office.

2. A proposal for the amendment of this Constitution under this Article shall not be enacted into law if, prior to such enactment, the President, after consultation with the Council of State, shall have signified in a message under his hand and Seal addressed to the Chairman of each of

Article 51 *(contd.)*

the Houses of the Oireachtas that the proposal is in his opinion a proposal to effect an amendment of such a character and importance that the will of the people thereon ought to be ascertained by Referendum before its enactment into law.

3. The foregoing provisions of this Article shall cease to have the force of law immediately upon the expiration of the period of three years referred to in section 1 hereof.

4. This Article shall be omitted from every official text of this Constitution published after the expiration of the said period.

TRANSITORY PROVISIONS.

Article 52.

1. This Article and subsequent Articles shall be omitted from every official text of this Constitution published after the date on which the first President shall have entered upon his office.

2. Every Article of this Constitution which is hereafter omitted in accordance with the foregoing provisions of this Article from the official text of this Constitution shall notwithstanding such omission continue to have the force of law.

TRANSITORY PROVISIONS.

Article 53.

1. On the coming into operation of this Constitution a general election for Seanad Éireann shall be held in accordance with the relevant Articles of this Constitution as if a dissolution of Dáil Éireann had taken place on the date of the coming into operation of this Constitution.

2. For the purposes of this Article references in the relevant provisions of this Constitution to a dissolution of Dáil Éireann shall be construed as referring to the coming into operation of this Constitution, and in those provisions the expression "Dáil Éireann" shall include the Chamber of Deputies (Dáil Éireann) established by the Constitution hereby repealed.

Article 53 *(contd.)*

3. The first assembly of Seanad Éireann shall take place not later than one hundred and eighty days after the coming into operation of this Constitution.

TRANSITORY PROVISIONS.

Article 54.

1. The Chamber of Deputies (Dáil Éireann) established by the Constitution hereby repealed and existing immediately before that repeal shall, on the coming into operation of this Constitution, become and be Dáil Éireann for all the purposes of this Constitution.

2. Every person who is a member of the said Chamber of Deputies (Dáil Éireann) immediately before the said repeal shall, on the coming into operation of this Constitution, become and be a member of Dáil Éireann as if he had been elected to be such member at an election held under this Constitution.

Article 54 *(contd.)*

3. The member of the said Chamber of Deputies (Dáil Éireann) who is immediately before the said repeal Ceann Comhairle shall upon the coming into operation of this Constitution become and be the Chairman of Dáil Éireann.

TRANSITORY PROVISIONS.

Article 55.

1. After the coming into operation of this Constitution and until the first assembly of Seanad Éireann, the Oireachtas shall consist of one House only.

2. The House forming the Oireachtas under this Article shall be Dáil Éireann.

3. Until the first President enters upon his office, the Oireachtas shall be complete and capable of functioning notwithstanding that there is no President.

4. Until the first President enters upon his office, bills passed or deemed to have been passed by the House or by both Houses of the Oireachtas shall be signed and promulgated by the Commission hereinafter mentioned instead of by the President.

TRANSITORY PROVISIONS.

Article 56.

1. On the coming into operation of this Constitution, the Government in office immediately before the coming into operation of this Constitution shall become and be the Government for the purposes of this Constitution and the members of that Government shall without any appointment under Article 13 hereof, continue to hold their respective offices as if they had been appointed thereto under the said Article 13.

2. The members of the Government in office on the date on which the first President shall enter upon his office shall receive official appointments from the President as soon as may be after the said date.

Article 56 *(contd.)*

3. The Departments of State of Saorstát Éireann shall as on and from the date of the coming into operation of this Constitution and until otherwise determined by law become and be the Departments of State.

4. On the coming into operation of this Constitution, the Civil Service of the Government of Saorstát Éireann shall become and be the Civil Service of the Government.

5. 1°[91] Nothing in this Constitution shall prejudice or affect the ~~terms, conditions, remuneration or tenure~~ terms and conditions of service, or the tenure of office or the remuneration[92] of any person who was in any Governmental employment immediately prior to the coming into operation of this Constitution.

    2° Nothing in this Article shall operate to invalidate or restrict any legislation whatsoever which has been enacted or may be enacted hereafter applying to or prejudicing or affecting all or any of the matters contained in the next preceding sub-section.[93]

---

91. Second Amendment of the Constitution Act, 1941, Ref. No. 30.
92. Second Amendment of the Constitution Act, 1941, Ref. No. 29.
93. Second Amendment of the Constitution Act, 1941, Ref. No. 30.

TRANSITORY PROVISIONS.

Article 57.

1. The first President shall enter upon his office not later than one hundred and eighty days after the date of the coming into operation of this Constitution.

2. After the date of the coming into operation of this Constitution and pending the entry of the first President upon his office the powers and functions of the President under this Constitution shall be exercised by a Commission consisting of the following persons, namely, the Chief Justice, the President of the High Court, and the Chairman of Dáil Éireann.

3. Whenever the Commission is incomplete by reason of a vacancy in an office the holder of which is a member of

Article 57 *(contd.)*

the Commission, the Commission shall, during such vacancy, be completed by the substitution of the senior judge of the Supreme Court who is not already a member of the Commission in the place of the holder of such office, and likewise in the event of any member of the Commission being, on any occasion, unable to act, his place shall be taken on that occasion by the senior judge of the Supreme Court who is available and is not already a member, or acting in the place of a member, of the Commission.

4.   The Commission may act by any two of their number.

5.   The provisions of this Constitution which relate to the exercise and performance by the President of the powers and functions conferred on him by this Constitution shall apply to the exercise and performance of the said powers and functions by the said Commission in like manner as those provisions apply to the exercise and performance of the said powers and functions by the President.

TRANSITORY PROVISIONS.

Article 58.

1. On and after the coming into operation of this Constitution and until otherwise determined by law, the Supreme Court of Justice, the High Court of Justice, the Circuit Court of Justice and the District Court of Justice in existence immediately before the coming into operation of this Constitution shall, subject to the provisions of this Constitution relating to the determination of questions as to the validity of any law, continue to exercise the same jurisdictions respectively as theretofore, and any judge or justice being a member of any such Court shall, subject to compliance with the subsequent provisions of this Article, continue to be a member thereof and shall hold office by the like tenure and on the like terms as theretofore unless he signifies to the Taoiseach his desire to resign.

Article 58 *(contd.)*

2. Every such judge and justice who shall not have so signified his desire to resign shall make and subscribe the declaration set forth in section 5 of Article 34 of this Constitution.

3. This declaration shall be made and subscribed by the Chief Justice in the presence of the Taoiseach, and by each of the other judges of the said Supreme Court, the judges of the said High Court and the judges of the said Circuit Court in the presence of the Chief Justice in open court.

4. In the case of the justices of the said District Court the declaration shall be made and subscribed in open court.

5. Every such declaration shall be made immediately upon the coming into operation of this Constitution, or as soon as may be thereafter.

6. Any such judge or justice who declines or neglects to make such declaration in the manner aforesaid shall be deemed to have vacated his office.

TRANSITORY PROVISIONS.

Article 59.

On the coming into operation of this Constitution, the person who is the Attorney General of Saorstát Éireann immediately before the coming into operation of this Constitution shall, without any appointment under Article 30 of this Constitution, become and be the Attorney General as if he had been appointed to that office under the said Article 30.

TRANSITORY PROVISIONS.

Article 60.

On the coming into operation of this Constitution the person who is the Comptroller and Auditor General of Saorstát Éireann immediately before the coming into operation of this Constitution shall, without any appointment under Article 33 of this Constitution, become and be the Comproller and Auditor General as if he had been appointed to that office under the said Article 33.

TRANSITORY PROVISIONS.

Article 61.

1. On the coming into operation of this Constitution, the Defence Forces and the Police Forces of Saorstát Éireann in existence immediately before the coming into operation of this Constitution shall become and be respectively the Defence Forces and the Police Forces of the State.

2. 1° Every commissioned officer of the Defence Forces of Saorstát Éireann immediately before the coming into operation of this Constitution shall become and be a commissioned officer of corresponding rank of the Defence Forces of the State as if he had received a commission therein under Article 13 of this Constitution.

Article 61 *(contd.)*

2° Every officer of the Defence Forces of the State at the date on which the first President enters upon his office shall receive a commission from the President as soon as may be after that date.

TRANSITORY PROVISIONS.

Article 62.

This Constitution shall come into operation

i.   on the day following the expiration of a period of one hundred and eighty days after its approval by the people signified by a majority of the votes cast at a plebiscite thereon held in accordance with law, or,

ii. on such earlier day after such approval as may be fixed by a resolution of Dáil Éireann elected at the general election the polling for which shall have taken place on the same day as the said plebiscite.

TRANSITORY PROVISIONS.

Article 63.

A copy of this Constitution signed by the Taoiseach, the Chief Justice, and the Chairman of Dáil Éireann, shall be enrolled for record in the office of the Registrar of the Supreme Court, and such signed copy shall be conclusive evidence of the provisions of this Constitution. In case of conflict between the Irish and the English texts, the Irish text shall prevail.

Dochum Glóire Dé
agus
Onóra na hÉireann.

The Amending Acts
and Oireachtas Debates

This part of the book discusses and provides the texts of the Acts to amend the Constitution, extracts from the Oireachtas debates and the outcome of the referenda where appropriate.

FIRST AMENDMENT ACT — OIREACHTAS DEBATES

The First Amendment of the Constitution Bill, 1939, was introduced and passed by both houses of the Oireachtas on 2 September 1939. As the Bill was introduced within the transitory period set out in Article 51 of the Constitution, there was no referendum on the Bill which became part of the Constitution on the signature of the President.

DÁIL ÉIREANN

The Bill was introduced in the Dáil at 3 p.m. and much of the subsequent debate was less concerned with the Amendment Bill than with the Emergency Powers Bill, 1939, also going through that day. The Taoiseach, Eamon de Valera, sought leave to introduce the Bill which passed from the First Stage directly to the Second Stage. He explained the need for the Bill when he was introducing it:

> 'some doubt was expressed by legal officers as to whether "time of war" might not be narrowly interpreted by courts to mean a time in which the State was actually a participant, a belligerent . . . we are, under that assumption, extending the meaning to be that which, I think, everybody would reasonably expect it to cover when we were passing the Constitution.'

Leave to introduce the Bill was granted without reply or division. At the Second Stage some desiderata were expressed. Deputy Cosgrave[94] said:

> 'It would be desirable that some provision should be inserted in this amendment of the Constitution providing for proof that there is an armed conflict affecting the vital interests of this country.'

---

94. William Thomas Cosgrave: Born in Dublin in 1880; Minister for Local Government, 1918-22; President of the Executive Council, 1922-32.

Deputy McGilligan added:

> 'I think that the Taoiseach will get more confidence
> here and now in the moderation he intends to use with
> regard to these proposals, if he will give the guarantees
> I have requested, and state that the liberty and right to
> discuss will be forthcoming.'

But the whole tenor of the debate was captured by Deputy
Dillon:

> 'reluctant though we may be to give these Draconian
> powers, I think we are obliged to give them . . . '

By 4 p.m. the Bill had passed all stages and gone to the
Seanad.

SEANAD ÉIREANN

The First Amendment of the Constitution Bill, 1939, was
introduced in the Seanad at 4.15 p.m. on 2 September 1939
by de Valera, in very much the same terms as he had
introduced it in the Dáil. The debate was in large measure
concerned with the issue of neutrality, which most
favoured, and with the issues raised by the associated
National Emergency motion which was taken the same day.
There was some support for favouring the democracies
while other speakers were anxious that the emergency
powers being sought should not be abused. To the latter the
Taoiseach replied:

> 'I do not think it is within the wit of man to devise a
> phrase which will prevent, in certain circumstances, an
> unscrupulous majority from betraying its democratic
> obligations and overturning democracy if it considers
> itself strong enough to do so.'

In the end the debate was brief. The Bill passed all its Seanad stages and the Seanad adjourned at 5.50 p.m. to resume at 6.30 p.m. to discuss the National Emergency motion. The Bill was signed that evening by the President.

FIRST AMENDMENT OF THE CONSTITUTION ACT, 1939

AN ACT TO AMEND THE CONSTITUTION
[*2 September 1939*]
[under Article 51]

WHEREAS by virtue of Article 46 of the Constitution any provision of the Constitution may be amended in the manner provided by that Article:

AND WHEREAS it is provided by Article 51 of the Constitution that any of the provisions of the Constitution may, subject as thereinafter provided, be amended by the Oireachtas within a period of three years after the date on which the first President shall have entered upon his office:

AND WHEREAS the first President entered upon his office on the 25th day of June, 1938:

AND WHEREAS sub-section 3° of section 3 of Article 28 of the Constitution is as follows:,

'3°   Nothing in this Constitution shall be invoked to invalidate any law enacted by the Oireachtas which is expressed to be for the purpose of securing the public safety and the preservation of the State in time of war or armed rebellion, or to nullify any act done or purporting to be done in pursuance of any such law.'

AND WHEREAS it is proposed that the Constitution be amended by inserting the following words at the end of and as part of sub-section 3° of section 3 of Article 28, that is to say:

'In this sub-section "time of war" includes a time when there is taking place an armed conflict in which the

State is not a participant but in respect of which each of the Houses of the Oireachtas shall have resolved that, arising out of such armed conflict, a national emergency exists affecting the vital interests of the State.'

BE IT THEREFORE ENACTED BY THE OIREACHTAS AS FOLLOWS:

1. Upon the passing of this Act the said proposed amendment of the Constitution shall forthwith become and be effective and the following words, that is to say:

   'In this sub-section "time of war" includes a time when there is taking place an armed conflict in which the State is not a participant but in respect of which each of the Houses of the Oireachtas shall have resolved that, arising out of such armed conflict, a national emergency exists affecting the vital interests of the State.'

   shall be inserted at the end of and as part of sub-section $3°$ of section 3 of Article 28 of the Constitution.

2. (1) The amendment of the Constitution effected by this Act shall be known as and may for all purposes be referred to as the First Amendment of the Constitution.

   (2) This Act may be cited as the First Amendment of the Constitution Act, 1939.

SECOND AMENDMENT ACT— OIREACHTAS DEBATES

DÁIL ÉIREANN

The Second Amendment of the Constitution Bill, 1940, was introduced in Dáil Éireann on 27 November 1940 by the Taoiseach, Eamon de Valera. The debate in both Houses was held during a crucial period in the War but it is still interesting that there was relatively little public comment. *The Irish Times* carried reports of the debate but without comment, although it did find the space to comment on strikes in the USA, the 10 oz tea ration, the laying up of motor cars and secondary education.

On 2 April 1941 the Second Stage was introduced. In his speech on the Bill the Taoiseach said:

> 'The majority of these amendments are not of fundamental importance . . . There are, however, two or three amendments which are of a more important type . . . [concerning emergency powers, *habeas corpus* and transferred officers] . . . there is the obvious desirability of keeping those [emergency] powers for some while longer, because there is no doubt that immediately after the war you do not quite get back to a position of peace . . . '

The tone of the Opposition approach was set by Professor O'Sullivan:

> 'except for the rather amusing light thrown on certain mischances and misadventures of the Constitution, I cannot see any great importance in these proposals.'

Indicative of the debate is the following exchange:

Deputy Norton: Article 56 still survives.

Deputy Dillon: My copy has 51 Articles.

Taoiseach: If you want to get the transitory Articles you have to get an early edition, before they were spent. They are spent as far as the Constitution is concerned.

Deputy Norton: I take it that the amendment here on pages 22 and 23 set out to amend Article 56. Would the Taoiseach agree with that?

Taoiseach: That is right, because it has the force of law.

General Mulcahy: It is a Bill to amend the Constitution.

Deputy Dillon: It is like the Cheshire cat.

Deputy Dillon also made the point that:

> 'There have been 28 amendments in the light of 18 months' experience. I wonder, at the end of another 18 months, will the Taoiseach be longing to apply 28 more rags and patches to the patchwork quilt which he will then have placed us in possession of?'

And he concluded:

> 'It is not Constitutions and orders that require amendment in our day, but rather the hearts of men.'

The Bill passed the Second Stage by 57 votes to 41.

On 24 April 1941, the Committee Stage began. One of the problems which was highlighted by the Bill was the question of the Bill being debated in a language which did not have priority of interpretation. Professor O'Sullivan asked:

'Suppose the two texts disagree. Surely it is the English text that ought to be amended to bring it into harmony with the fundamental text passed by the House and not vice-versa . . . It might seem as if we had passed the English text and that the Irish text is a translation, which is something I find it extremely difficult to believe . . . The whole Constitution is a splendid example of anacoluthon.'

There was considerable debate about the preparing of official texts by the Taoiseach and the signing of prepared texts of the Constitution by the President.

With regard to item no. 15 Deputy Costello said:

'The object of the proposal in the Bill is to ensure that there shall be only one judgment delivered by the Supreme Court . . . I do not agree that it is desirable that there should be only one judgment in a matter of this kind.'

The Taoiseach replied:

'It is desirable in the case of the Constitution to have finality, and it is thought that this will be best secured by a single judgment.'

Deputy Costello returned to the question:

'A dissentient judgement on Constitutional matters may be as valuable from the point of views of Constitutional theory and the stimulation of Constitutional thought as the judgment of the majority; in fact, sometimes it may be very much more valuable.'

The Taoiseach did not accept the point:

'There is a great deal to be said for the point of view he [Deputy Costello] put forward about stimulus to thought and so on, but that is not the purpose of sending a case to the Supreme Court.'

Regarding item no. 22 Professor O'Sullivan made the following point:

'What I object to is a completely undefined and unlimited extension of what I might call, I think without exaggeration, the suspension of what remains of the guarding Articles of the Constitution so far as personal liberty is concerned.'

The Taoiseach was conciliatory:

'I shall consider it. As I told the House at the start, I very much dislike the indefiniteness, but the only thing is that you are not going to make it more definite without running very great risks.'

The Bill passed the Committee Stage.

Amendments introduced at the Report Stage, on 1 May 1941, removed an apparent compulsion on the President to sign any purported official text of the Constitution, clarified the position regarding acts done in time of war or armed rebellion, specified that an emergency ceases to exist only after resolutions by both Houses and allowed certain courts to be held in camera. On the general question of the details which had been discussed throughout the debate the Taoiseach remarked:

'The Constitution can only be generally directive, except in a few special cases. If you are going to treat the Constitution as an Act of Parliament in which you will have every possible case that you can think of covered, then you will not have a Constitution in the ordinary sense at all.'

The Report Stage passed.

During the debate on the Fifth Stage on 7 May 1941, there was a major exchange between Deputy McGilligan and the Taoiseach. Deputy McGilligan said:

'Constitutions were supposed to be drawn with certain fundamental rights so protective that the process of law could not take away those fundamental rights or could not whittle them down to a point when they were negligible . . . The progress under the Constitution that we are discussing has been towards making law superior to the Constitution. The progress right along since the Constitution was introduced has been to make the Constitution itself subservient to the ordinary law, and the ordinary law, of course, is passed by a simple majority. That progress is still further marked by the amendments . . . There is observable here the tendency—which is usual with loosely-worded documents—that, instead of tying the hands of the Executive, great care is taken, in the First Amendment of the Constitution, to increase that power; and again, in the Second Amendment of the Constitution, care is taken to extend it still further and to increase the power of the Executive by making it more supreme. It appears that, once an emergency has been voted, it requires positive action on the part of this House to bring that emergency period to a close, in order that the Constitution may again be operative as far as the courts of this country are concerned.'

The Taoiseach responded:

'I think it would be quite impossible for us to produce any document of a reasonable size which would even cover some of the cases that might suggest themselves to any person who throws himself in imagination into the possible difficulties that might arise and the possible cases that might arise. On the whole, we have to take the position that a body of representatives who have been elected by the people will ordinarily act in good faith and if the situation is reached in which they are prepared to abuse their position and abuse their power to the extent that it is suggested when we are asked to amend these Articles in definite ways, then there is an end to popular representation in the ordinary way; a new situation is come about; you are practically into a revolutionary situation in which a coup has been effected by the Executive, because that is what it would practically mean.'

The Bill was put and declared carried.

SEANAD ÉIREANN

The Second Amendment of the Constitution Bill, 1940, was introduced in the Seanad on 14 May 1941. The discussion that followed was largely about the Constitution itself, which some Senators felt they had lost out on debating. As the Taoiseach remarked:

'The amendments that are proposed are perhaps, in the main, not of fundamental importance. A great number of them are intended merely to clarify or improve the text and in one or two cases to remedy oversights.'

The two amendments around which he thought the debate would centre were no. 22, the emergency, and no. 27, *habeas corpus*. In this the Taoiseach was mistaken, the principal point made in the debate was that the Constitution was unfortunate in root and branch, and that no amount of tinkering would be of assistance. Thus Senator M. Hayes:

'My principal difficulty about this Constitution (Amendment) Bill is that the amendments are of a very minor character and that what appear to me to be the real problems of the Constitution and the real amendments required have not been introduced at all . . . For example, the Preamble to the Constitution says: "We, the people of Éire . . . adopt, enact, and give to ourselves this Constitution." The name "Éire" is most unfortunate and the people who adopted it were not the people of Éire but the people of Saorstát Éireann.'

Other issues raised included the fact that the panels for Seanad elections had been fixed before the Commission on Vocational Organisation had the opportunity of reporting on the matter, the increase in power the amendment would give to the Executive, the continuation of the Emergency until the Oireachtas otherwise decides, the superiority of the Constitution enacted in 1922, that in a time of crisis 'piffling around with these constitutional matters would hardly appeal to anybody', and the assertion of Parliamentary Sovereignty made by Desmond FitzGerald who said:

'In the document itself and in the speeches relating to it, it was stated that the ultimate law-making power was the people. We in this legislature have here that authority. It does not exist in the multitude . . . It says: "All powers of government, legislative, executive and judicial, derive, under God, from the people . . ." Personally and philosophically I disagree with the statement . . . it is a metaphysical absurdity to suggest that authority can have as subject a multiplicity.'

Professor Tierney made the more radical point:

'Our ancestors whether they got on well or ill, got on for several thousand years before they ever heard of the word Constitution or knew anything about Constitutions. The whole idea of the Constitution . . . is an illusion that in its essence should be totally foreign to the realist, sensible people of this country.'

In this he was contradicted by Peadar Mac Fhionnlaoich's confident assertion:

'Is é mo bharúil go bhfuil furmhór na ndaoine san tír sásta, no go measardha sásta, leis an Bhunreacht, gidh go mbéidir go mbeidh leasú ag teastail anois agus arís.'

The Second stage was passed and the Bill entered the Committee Stage on 21 May 1941. Here the discussion covered the Irish text, corporative organisation, the single judgment without dissenting judgment of the Supreme Court and the indefinite duration of the state of emergency. The Bill completed its Committee Stage. The Report and Final Stages were taken on 27 May 1941 and all stages passed.

NOTE
The reader will notice that the Second Amendment Act contains changes to the Irish text for which there is no corresponding change in the English text. This situation arose because the Constitution Bill was debated in English and amendments as they were accepted were subsequently translated into Irish (although the Irish text maintained its legal primacy), and some such changes were not carried through. For example, in Article 18.4.3 the Draft Bill said that 'Forty-three shall be elected by the electorate hereinafter specified from panels of candidates constituted as hereinafter provided'. The Act as passed said 'Forty-three shall be elected from panels of candidates constituted as hereinafter provided', but made only spelling changes in the

Irish text. The Second Amendment of the Constitution Act, Ref. No. 7 brought them into line.

SECOND AMENDMENT OF THE CONSTITUTION ACT, 1941

AN ACT TO AMEND THE CONSTITUTION
[*30 May 1941*]
[under Article 51]

WHEREAS by virtue of Article 46 of the Constitution any provision of the Constitution may be amended in the manner provided by that Article:

AND WHEREAS it is provided by Article 51 of the Constitution that any of the provisions of the Constitution may, subject as thereinafter provided, be amended by the Oireachtas within a period of three years after the date on which the first President shall have entered upon his office:

AND WHEREAS the first President entered upon his office on the 25th day of June, 1938:

AND WHEREAS experience has shown that certain amendments of the Constitution are desirable:

AND WHEREAS it is therefore proposed that the several amendments of the Irish text and the English text respectively of the Constitution which are set out in the Schedule to this Act should be made by the Oireachtas:

BE IT THEREFORE ENACTED BY THE OIREACHTAS AS FOLLOWS:

1. Upon the passing of this Act the several amendments of the Irish text and the English text respectively of the Constitution which are specified in the Schedule to this Act shall forthwith become and be effective and, for that

purpose, every Article of the Constitution mentioned in the second column of the said Schedule shall

(*a*) as respects the Irish text thereof, be amended in the manner stated in the third column of the said Schedule opposite the mention, or each of the several mentions, of the Article in the said second column, and

(*b*) as respects the English text thereof, be amended in the manner stated in the fourth column of the said Schedule opposite the mention, or each of the several mentions, of the Article in the said second column.

2. (1) The several amendments of the Constitution effected by this Act shall be collectively known as and may for all purposes be collectively referred to as the Second Amendment of the Constitution, and any particular one of those amendments may, for purposes of identification, be referred to by the number in the first column of the Schedule to this Act opposite the statement of such amendment in the other columns of this said Schedule.

(2) This Act may be cited as the Second Amendment of the Constitution Act, 1941.

SCHEDULE
Particulars of Amendments

Ref. No.	Article amended	Nature of amendment of the English text
1	Article 11	No corresponding amendment.
2	Article 12	In sub-section 3° of section 3, the insertion of the words and brackets '(whether occurring before or after he enters upon his office)' immediately after the words 'as aforesaid'.
3	Article 13	No corresponding amendment.
4	Article 14	The deletion of the words 'by this Constitution' where they occur in section 1, in section 4, in sub-section 1° of section 5, and in sub-section 2° of section 5, and the insertion in each case of the words 'by or under this Constitution' in the place of the said deleted words.
5	Article 15	No corresponding amendment.
6	Article 18	In section 3, the deletion of the words 'nominated by the Taoiseach with their prior consent', and the insertion in their place of the words 'nominated, with their prior consent, by the Taoiseach who is appointed next after the reassembly of Dáil Éireann following the dissolution thereof which occasions the nomination of the said members'.
7	Article 18	No corresponding amendment.
8	Article 20	No corresponding amendment.

9	Article 24	The deletion of section 2 and the insertion in its place of a new section as follows, that is to say:
		'2. Where a Bill, the time for the consideration of which by Seanad Éireann has been abridged under this Article,
		(a) is, in the case of a Bill which is not a Money Bill, rejected by Seanad Éireann or passed by Seanad Éireann with amendments to which Dáil Éireann does not agree or neither passed nor rejected by Seanad Éireann, or
		(b) is, in the case of a Money Bill, either returned by Seanad Éireann to Dáil Éireann with recommendations which Dáil Éireann does not accept or is not returned by Seanad Éireann to Dáil Éireann,
		within the period specified in the resolution, the Bill shall be deemed to have been passed by both Houses of the Oireachtas at the expiration of that period.'
10	Article 25	In sub-section 1° of section 2, the deletion of the word 'five' and the insertion in its place of the words 'the fifth', and the deletion of the words 'seven days' and the insertion in their place of the words 'the seventh day'; in subsection 2° of section 2, the deletion of the words 'five days' and the insertion in their place of the words 'the fifth day'.

11	Article 25	The deletion of section 4 and the insertion in its place of a new section as follows, that is to say:

'4. 1° Every Bill shall become and be law as on and from the day on which it is signed by the President under this Constitution, and shall, unless the contrary intention appears, come into operation on that day.

2° Every Bill signed by the President under this Constitution shall be promulgated by him as a law by the publication by his direction of a notice in the *Iris Oifigiúil* stating that the Bill has become law.

3° Every Bill shall be signed by the President in the text in which it was passed or deemed to have been passed by both Houses of the Oireachtas, and if a Bill is so passed or deemed to have been passed in both the official languages, the President shall sign the text of the Bill in each of those languages.

4° Where the President signs the text of a Bill in one only of the official languages, an official translation shall be issued in the other official language.

5° As soon as may be after the signature and promulgation of a Bill as a law, the text of such law

11	Article 25 *(contd.)*	which was signed by the President or, where the President has signed the text of such law in each of the official languages, both the signed texts shall be enrolled for record in the office of the Registrar of the Supreme Court, and the text, or both the texts, so enrolled shall be conclusive evidence of the provisions of such law. 6° In case of conflict between the texts of a law enrolled under this section in both the official languages, the text in the national language shall prevail.'
12	Article 25	The addition of a new section (at the end of the Article) as follows, that is to say: '5. 1° It shall be lawful for the Taoiseach, from time to time as occasion appears to him to require, to cause to be prepared under his supervision a text (in both the official languages) of this Constitution as then in force embodying all amendments theretofore made therein. 2° A copy of every text so prepared, when authenticated by the signatures of the Taoiseach and the Chief Justice, shall be signed by the President and shall be enrolled for record in the office of the Registrar of the Supreme Court.

12	Article 25 (contd.)	3° The copy so signed and enrolled which is for the time being the latest text so prepared shall, upon such enrolment, be conclusive evidence of this Constitution as at the date of such enrolment and shall for that purpose supersede all texts of this Constitution of which copies were previously so enrolled. 4° In case of conflict between the texts of any copy of this Constitution enrolled under this section, the text in the national language shall prevail.'
13	Article 26	In sub-section 2° of section 1, the deletion of the words 'four days' and the insertion in their place of the words 'the seventh day'.
14	Article 26	In sub-section 2° of section 1, the deletion of the words 'passed or deemed to have been passed by both Houses of the Oireachtas' and the insertion in their place of the words 'presented by the Taoiseach to the President for his signature'.
15	Article 26	The addition at the end of sub-section 2° of section 2 of the words 'and shall be pronounced by such one of those judges as the Court shall direct, and no other opinion, whether assenting or dissenting, shall be pronounced nor shall the existence of any such other opinion be disclosed'.

16	Article 26	In section 3, the insertion, immediately before sub-section 2° thereof, of a new sub-section as follows, that is to say:
		'2° If, in the case of a Bill to which Article 27 of this Constitution applies, a petition has been addressed to the President under that Article, that Article shall be complied with.'
		And the alteration of the number of sub-section 2° of section 3 from '2°' to '3°'.
17	Article 27	The insertion, immediately before section 2, of a new section as follows, that is to say:
		'2. Every such petition shall be in writing and shall be signed by the petitioners whose signatures shall be verified in the manner prescribed by law.'
		And in section 2, the deletion of the words 'shall be in writing signed by the petitioners,'.
		And the alteration of the numbers of sections 2, 3, 4 and 5 respectively from those numbers to '3,' '4,' '5' and '6' respectively.
18	Article 27	The numbering of section 3 as sub-section 1° of that section, and the addition to the said section 3 of a new subsection as follows, that is to say:
		'2° If the Bill or any provision thereof is or has been referred to the

18	Article 27 *(contd.)*	Supreme Court under Article 26 of this Constitution, it shall not be obligatory on the President to consider the petition unless or until the Supreme Court has pronounced a decision on such reference to the effect that the said Bill or the said provision thereof is not repugnant to this Constitution or to any provision thereof, and, if a decision to that effect is pronounced by the Supreme Court, it shall not be obligatory on the President to pronounce his decision on the petition before the expiration of six days after the day on which the decision of the Supreme Court to the effect aforesaid is pronounced.'
19	Article 27	In sub-section 2° of section 4, the deletion of the words 'Every such Bill which' and the insertion in their place of the words 'Whenever a proposal contained in a Bill the subject of a petition under this Article', and the insertion, immediately after the word 'section,' of the words 'such Bill'.
20	Article 28	The insertion, in sub-section 3° of section 3, immediately before the words 'in pursuance of any such law' of the words 'in time of war or armed rebellion'.
21	Article 28	No corresponding amendment.

22	Article 28	The addition at the end of sub-section 3° of section 3, after the words inserted by the First Amendment of the Constitution, of the words 'and "time of war or armed rebellion" includes such time after the termination of any war, or of any such armed conflict as aforesaid, or of an armed rebellion, as may elapse until each of the Houses of the Oireachtas shall have resolved that the national emergency occasioned by such war, armed conflict, or armed rebellion has ceased to exist.'
23	Article 34	The deletion of section 1 and the insertion in its place of a new section as follows, that is to say:
		'1. Justice shall be administered in courts established by law by judges appointed in the manner provided by this Constitution, and, save in such special and limited cases as may be prescribed by law, shall be administered in public.'
24	Article 34	In section 3 the deletion of sub-section 2° and the insertion in its place of two new sub-sections as follows, that is to say:
		'2° Save as otherwise provided by this Article, the jurisdiction of the High Court shall extend to the question of the validity of any law having regard to the provisions of this Constitution, and no such question

24	Article 34 (contd.)	shall be raised (whether by pleading, argument or otherwise) in any Court established under this or any other Article of this Constitution other than the High Court or the Supreme Court.
		3° No Court whatever shall have jurisdiction to question the validity of a law, or any provision of a law, the Bill for which shall have been referred to the Supreme Court by the President under Article 26 of this Constitution, or to question the validity of a provision of a law where the corresponding provision in the Bill for such law shall have been referred to the Supreme Court by the President under the said Article 26.'
		And the alteration of the number of sub-section 3° of section 3 from '3°' to '4°'.
25	Article 34	In section 4, the insertion, immediately before sub-section 5° thereof, of a new sub-section as follows, that is to say:
		'5° The decision of the Supreme Court on a question as to the validity of a law having regard to the provisions of this Constitution shall be pronounced by such one of the judges of that Court as that Court shall direct, and no other opinion on such question, whether

25	Article 34 *(contd.)*	assenting or dissenting, shall be pronounced, nor shall the existence of any such other opinion be disclosed.'
		And the alteration of the number of sub-section 5° of section 4 from '5°' to '6°'.
26	Article 34	No corresponding amendment.
27	Article 40	In section 4, the deletion of sub-section 2° and the insertion in its place of four new sub-sections as follows, that is to say:
		'2° Upon complaint being made by or on behalf of any person to the High Court or any judge thereof alleging that such person is being unlawfully detained, the High Court and any and every judge thereof to whom such complaint is made shall forthwith enquire into the said complaint and may order the person in whose custody such person is detained to produce the body of such person before the High Court on a named day and to certify in writing the grounds of his detention, and the High Court shall, upon the body of such person being produced before that Court and after giving the person in whose custody he is detained an opportunity of justifying the detention, order the release of such person from such detention

27   Article 40
     (contd.)

unless satisfied that he is being detained in accordance with the law.

3° Where the body of a person alleged to be unlawfully detained is produced before the High Court in pursuance of an order in that behalf made under this section and that Court is satisfied that such person is being detained in accordance with a law but that such law is invalid having regard to the provisions of this Constitution, the High Court shall refer the question of the validity of such law to the Supreme Court by way of case stated and may, at the time or such reference or at any time thereafter, allow the said person to be at liberty on such bail and subject to such conditions as the High Court shall fix until the Supreme Court has determined the question so referred to it.

4° The High Court before which the body of a person alleged to be unlawfully detained is to be produced in pursuance of an order in that behalf made under this section shall, if the President of the High Court or, if he is not available, the senior judge of that Court who is available so directs in respect of any particular case, consist of three judges and shall, in every other case, consist of one judge only.

27	Article 40 *(contd.)*	5° Where an order is made under this section by the High Court or a judge thereof for the production of the body of a person who is under sentence of death, the High Court or such judge thereof shall further order that the execution of the said sentence of death shall be deferred until after the body of such person has been produced before the High Court and the lawfulness of his detention has been determined and if, after such deferment, the detention of such person is determined to be lawful, the High Court shall appoint a day for the execution of the said sentence of death and that sentence shall have effect with the substitution of the day so appointed for the day originally fixed for the execution thereof.' And the alteration of the number of sub-section 3° of section 4 from '3'' to '6''.
28	Article 47	In section 2, the deletion of the words 'Every Bill and' where they occur at the beginning of sub-section 1° and also where they occur at the beginning of sub-section 2°.
29	Article 56	In section 5, the deletion of the words 'terms, conditions, remuneration or tenure' and the insertion in their place of the words "terms and conditions of service, or the tenure of office or the remuneration'.

30	Article 56	The numbering of section 5 as sub-section 1° of that section, and the addition to the said section 5 of a new sub-section as follows, that is to say:
		'2° Nothing in this Article shall operate to invalidate or restrict any legislation whatsoever which has been enacted or may be enacted hereafter applying to or prejudicing or affecting all or any of the matters contained in the next preceding subsection.'

THIRD AMENDMENT ACT — OIREACHTAS DEBATES

DÁIL ÉIREANN

Dáil Éireann granted leave to the Taoiseach Jack Lynch to introduce the Third Amendment of the Constitution Bill, 1971, on 23 November 1971. The purpose of the Amendment was to enable Ireland to join the European Economic Community. (Already on the order paper was a Labour Party private members' Bill with the same title proposing to lower the voting age. That became the Fourth Amendment of the Constitution Bill. It did not pass.) The Second Stage began on 2 December 1971. The Bill was a major step in the process of deciding on membership of the European Communities and on the amendment of the Constitution which membership of the Communities required. There is a strong impression in the record of the debate that the Dáil was attempting to come to grips, almost for the first time, with the fact that we have a constitution. The debate did not discuss the merits of membership of the EEC. That subject was dealt with later in the debate on the White Paper on membership. The position was put plainly by the Taoiseach when introducing the Bill:

> 'What we shall be dealing with in debating this Bill is the nature of the Constitutional amendment which will be necessary in order to enable the State to undertake the obligations of membership of the Communities and, arising from this, the form of the question to be put to the people in the proposed referendum.'

The opposition Fine Gael party was in favour of entry into the EEC. In his reply to the Taoiseach, Justin Keating, on behalf of the Labour Party which was opposing entry to the EEC, said:

'we have the extraordinary situation whereby something that is absolutely fundamental not only to our Constitution but to the whole direction of our nation is being decided by the essential kernel of the Bill which consists of eleven lines and two sentences.'

He said he would have preferred to have had the consequences of signing the Treaties spelled out and incorporated into the specific Articles they affected. According to the Taoiseach the Government had considered this solution:

'The answer is that the Government consider that it would not be practicable to do so because the extent to which the Constitution would need to be amended is in the final analysis a matter for decision by the appropriate courts.'

Keating also objected to the phrase 'consequent upon' in the Bill which he had been advised was bad law on the grounds of legal vagueness. He said that the U.S. Supreme Court had accepted legal vagueness as grounds for striking down legislation and said:

'I understand also that at a certain level lawyers in all countries try to converge in their methods, in their standards and in their attitudes and that what is a good argument in an evolved and in some ways democratic nation like the United States, while not automatically applicable here, would at least have some force with lawyers in this country. It is proper that that should be so.'

It was the generality of the amendment to which he was objecting as he feared the amendment would have serious consequences for Irish neutrality.

'It is inconceivable that there will not be a European Army and that we will not be required to contribute to that Army.'

Dr Thornley, also for the Labour Party, was concerned with the looseness of language of the amendment and read the text of the amendment into the record. Being in favour of the Bill the Fine Gael party obviously took a different view. Thus Deputy Cosgrave:

'At the outset I want it to be clearly understood that we favour a referendum . . . Consequently, we approve the task of putting clearly before the electorate in simple language a single question as to whether or not this country adheres to the European Economic Community.'

He made the point that:

'There are a number of things in the Constitution which are good and as Deputy Keating rightly said most of them were taken from the 1922 Constitution which was drafted by constitutional experts under the chairmanship of Michael Collins . . . '

but he also took up the threat to neutrality:

'An absolute assurance should be given to the House and the country that no military or defence commitments of any character are involved.'

Other speakers also took up the issue of vagueness, what came to be called in the debate, 'a Constitutional blank cheque'. There was in fact quite an amount of uncertainty about the amendment. Barry Desmond referred to Senator Mary Robinson's[95] point that 'the proposed amendment is

---

95. Mary Robinson: Born in Mayo in 1944; Senior Counsel and university lecturer; Senator, 1969-89 for Dublin University; Labour Party candidate in various Dáil elections; introduced private members Bills on contraception, adoption, illegitimacy and domicile; President of CHERISH. Elected President of Ireland in November 1990.

extremely specific in its first part and unacceptably broad in its second part' and he went on to ask:

> 'Is it the case that the Constitution may, after accession to the Communities, only be amended in accordance with the Treaties themselves? Would it be necessary to have amendments of our own Constitution approved by the Court of Justice in Luxembourg or even by the executive institutions in Brussels?'

When the debate was resumed on 9 December 1971, other speakers took up the actual effects of EEC membership on industrial and commercial life, generally held to be favourable, but not always coherently. Some Labour deputies were lukewarm in their opposition to entry and Deputy M. O'Leary declared:

> 'We [in the Labour Party] consider that the conditions of true consultation with the people in a referendum on a supremely important matter are not best fulfilled in the form suggested in the Third Amendment. This is our only reason for opposing at this stage.'

Some Fine Gael deputies were not enthusiastically in favour of the Bill. Deputy T. J. Fitzpatrick attempted to put before the Dáil reasons why he believed the Bill as drafted, particularly the Schedule to it, was too vague for safety. But he was in favour of entry:

> 'Apart from economic reasons for entry, we have a national incentive in believing that entry into Europe will do away with the Border and make the artificial line between north and south of our country meaningless.'

The debate on the amendment was not particularly long as the White Paper had not yet been prepared to enable a comprehensive debate on the terms of accession to take place. The White Paper was expected in January. In his speech on the Second Stage the Taoiseach said:

'This Bill is confined to the constitutional means whereby accession to the European Economic Communities could be facilitated, first, if the terms of accession are agreeable to the Dáil and to the country and also, of course, if the people decide to make the necessary amendments to the Constitution that will enable us to take our part in the Community.'

The Taoiseach in his closing speech said that Deputy Keating had suggested that the Government was altering the fundamental rights of citizens, but that there was no foundation whatever for these suggestions. He summed up by saying:

'We see certain essential requirements for this type of amendment. First, it should be comprehensive enough to enable us to fulfil all the obligations required by the three Treaties and the great body of legislation that has flowed from them. As I said in my opening speech, the Supreme Court is competent to decide what Articles of the Constitution will be affected and that if we amend individual Articles, it will be very difficult to ensure that all the necessary amendments are carried out.'

The Second Stage was carried by 106 votes to 17. The Third Committee Stage was introduced on 25 January 1971. Deputy Cosgrave moved an amendment to delete the phrase 'consequent on' and substitute 'necessitated by the obligations of'. This amendment to the Bill was accepted by the Government on the grounds that it did not interfere with the Bill. This amendment was supported by Dr FitzGerald on the grounds that:

'If the Legislature passed a Bill of any kind expressed to be consequent on membership of the Community and if that Bill were, in the judgment of the Legislature, necessary, I am not at all sure that the High Court, or the Supreme Court, would look behind that to establish the facts, which is a matter for the Legislature given that the Bill is expressed to be consequent on membership.'

Dr Fitzgerald went on to say:

'The effect of changing these words is twofold . . . One is that it removes from our Government the power to introduce legislation which is not necessitated by the obligations of membership but which could be alleged or said to arise consequent on membership . . . It could [also] be argued that, if the words "consequent on membership" were left, a subsequent treaty negotiated for defence purposes between member states would be consequent on the three Treaties.'

Deputy Keating made a different and more fundamental point:

'We are being urged to consider this amendment entirely, to quote the Minister for Finance, as "referring specifically to three Treaties". This is legalistic and misleading and it is a serious point. We all know that the Communities are on-going things. Indeed, they have declared their future plans at some length. We know that Halstein formulation of many years ago: "We are not in business; we are in politics". There are many other statements. We get economic union, we get customs union, then we get economic union and a monetary union and then a political union.'

When the Committee Stage resumed on 26 January 1971, the amendment to the Bill was carried. No other amendments to the Bill were passed. Deputy Keating, who had been arguing for a looser associate relation with the EEC, concluded with the following words:

'For what it is worth, I put the prediction on the record that the common agricultural policy in its present form will not last five years, and the high food prices and the protected market for the sort of live-stock products we produce will not last five years in the Community.'

The question was carried by 75 votes to 9.

SEANAD ÉIREANN

On 24 February 1972, the Third Amendment of the Constitution Bill, 1971 was introduced in the Seanad. There was some anxiety displayed about neutrality and sovereignty. Once again the debate was restricted to matters directly affecting the Bill. Introducing it Deputy Andrews stressed that the Bill was intended to enable the State to undertake all the obligations of membership of the three existing European Communities, but only those obligations. The amendment was required primarily because provisions of the Constitution (i.e. Articles 6.2, 15.2, 29 and 34) were imcompatible with the application and implementation in this country of certain of the provisions of the Treaties of Rome and Paris and of implementing legislation enacted by the Communities or their institutions. Furthermore, he said the amendment should be in a form which would enable the electorate to answer a single question in the referendum by a simple 'yes' or 'no'. The 'blank cheque' argument was raised by Deputy J. Fitzgerald who added:

'I do not believe any of us can agree that we should ask the people to change or perhaps jettison the Constitution in this way.'

The Committee Stage began on 1 March 1972. It was largely dominated by the contributions of Professor John Kelly[96] and

---

96. Professor John Kelly: Born in Dublin in 1931; Senior Counsel and university professor; various ministerial appointments; Attorney General for Fine Gael. Author of *Fundamental Rights in the Irish Law and Constitution* and *The Irish Constitution*. Died in 1993.

Senator Mary Robinson. Professor Kelly raised the point that if a court:

'takes the view that this amendment to the Constitution, being part of the Constitution itself, will operate to rescue it then it is giving this part of the Constitution as amended by the people, as I hope they will amend it, a kind of primacy. I am not sure if the Government have grasped the extent of the primacy which they are according to this section because it is making it virtually impossible to cite any part of the Constitution—and this is where the difficulty of blanket amendment comes in—in order to challenge legislation which is overtly necessitated by membership of the European Economic Community.'

It followed that:

'the Oireachtas might find themselves in the position where they could deliberately delete something from the Constitution without going to the people at all, because this amendment does not confer any protective status on Article 46, which is the amending Article of the Constitution under which we are at present operating.'

Senator Robinson referred to the Public Safety Act, 1927 which amended the Constitution in so far as it was in conflict with any provision of the Act, and to *(The) Attorney General v McBride*, in 1928[97]. In that case Mr Justice Hanna stated:

'The question arises: Is it a sufficient compliance in law with Article 50 to insert in an Act of Parliament in vague and general terms a clause such as this—a drag-net—without specifying either any Article, or part of an

---

97. 1928 IR 456.

Article, of the Constitution that is to be amended, or
whether in fact any amendment is made? . . . The rights
of the people should not be obscured by the facile pen
of the parliamentary draughtsmen.'

Senator Robinson, arguing for the comprehensive
amendment of the Constitution, went on to say:

'The problem with this [Schedule] is that the
obligations now being assumed by member states of
the Communities go beyond the obligations of the
original Treaties.'

She gave examples of property law, international relations,
domestic budget harmonisation, environmental policy, etc.,
but she was the only speaker to express the view that the
amendment was too restrictive. She pointed out that a
decision was taken by the Council in March 1971 to
implement economic and monetary union and asked: 'What
happens when we go to implement that? What happens if
there is a challenge before our courts?' The answer, which
has been supported by the passage of time, was given on the
day by Senator E. Ryan:

'It should be recognised that there are two ways in
which we can deal with further steps which the
Communities want to take, such as those Senator
Robinson mentioned. First of all, if it is a really serious
step and a radical departure from what we are already
undertaking, it would be necessary to have a further
referendum . . . In so far as laws were necessary to
comply with them, the Oireachtas could pass laws
which would enable us to co-operate with the other
members of the Communities in effecting what was
necessary.'

The Bill was reported without amendment.

On 8 March 1972 the Report and Final Stages were taken. Senator Robinson proposed an amendment which read as follows:

> 'No provision of the Constitution invalidates laws enacted, acts done or measures adopted by the State either necessitated by the obligations of membership of the Communities or by policies adopted unanimously in the Council of Ministers of the Communities and given a legal basis by amendment of one of the aforesaid Treaties.'

But the Government had no intention of accepting this wording and the amendment was by leave withdrawn. Deputy Andrews, in reply to Senator Kelly, said:

> 'Nothing necessitated by membership will require further amendment of the Constitution and consequently an amendment of the Constitution by law will not and cannot arise from membership or will be necessitated by membership.'

In reply to the point raised by Senator Kelly that if a court takes the view that this amendment to the Constitution is giving this part of the Constitution a kind of primacy, Deputy Andrews said:

> 'I should also point out that it might be giving a first and second class type of status to various Articles of the Constitution and I think that would be a bad thing.'

The Bill passed without a division. It had passed the Seanad without amendment.

This was the first amendment of the Constitution to be passed by a referendum of the people. Polling took place on 10 May 1972.

As prescribed by the Electoral (Amendment) Act, 1972, the official polling card stated:

THE THIRD AMENDMENT OF THE CONSTITUTION BILL, 1971, proposes to add the subsection here following to Article 29.4 of the Constitution . . . [as per Schedule] . . . The purpose of the proposal is to allow the State to become a member of the Communities commonly known as European Communities.

Total electorate		1,783,604
Total poll		1,264,278
Percentage poll		70.9%
Votes in favour	1,041,890	[83.1%]
Votes against	211,891	[16.9%]
Spoiled votes		10,497

In no constituency was there a majority against the Bill. As the proposal was duly approved by the people, the Bill was signed by the President on 8 June 1972 and promulgated as law.

THIRD AMENDMENT OF THE CONSTITUTION ACT, 1972

AN ACT TO AMEND THE CONSTITUTION
[*8 June 1972*]

WHEREAS by virtue of Article 46 of the Constitution any provision of the Constitution may be amended in the manner provided by that Article:

AND WHEREAS it is proposed to amend Article 29 of the Constitution:

BE IT THEREFORE ENACTED BY THE OIREACHTAS AS FOLLOWS:

1. Article 29 of the Constitution is hereby amended as follows:
   (*a*) the subsection set out in *Part I* of this Schedule to this Act shall be added to section 4 of the Irish text,
   (*b*) the subsection set out in *Part II* of the Schedule to this Act shall be added to section 4 of the English text.

2. (1) The amendment of the Constitution effected by this Act shall be called the Third Amendment of the Constitution.

   (2) This Act may be cited as the Third Amendment of the Constitution Act, 1972.

SCHEDULE
Part II

3° The State may become a member of the European Coal and Steel Community (established by Treaty signed at Paris on the 18th day of April, 1951), the European Economic Community (established by Treaty signed at Rome on the 25th day of March, 1957) and the European Atomic Energy Community (established by Treaty signed at Rome on the 25th day of March, 1957). No provision of this Constitution invalidates laws enacted, acts done or measures adopted by the State necessitated by the obligations of membership of the Communities or prevents laws enacted, acts done or measures adopted by the Communities or institutions thereof, from having the force of law in the State.

FOURTH AMENDMENT ACTS — OIREACHTAS DEBATES

The Fourth Amendment of the Constitution Act 1972, was intended to give the vote to citizens over 18 years of age. As no member of the Oireachtas expressed opposition to the proposal, the debate was rather rambling.

DÁIL ÉIREANN

The Bill was introduced in the Dáil on 28 June 1972 by the Minister for Foreign Affairs, Dr Patrick Hillery. The entire Second Stage took place on 5 July 1972 when it was introduced by the Minister for Local Government, Deputy Molloy, in the following terms:

> 'I move that the Bill be now read a second time . . . This Bill proposes to amend the Constitution by reducing the voting age to 18 years . . . because the Constitution indicates that every Dáil elector has the right to vote at an election for President and at a referendum, the amendment will reduce the age for Presidential elections and referenda as well as for Dáil elections.'

Everyone who spoke was in favour of the Bill, some even arguing that it should have been extended to cover entry to the Oireachtas which remains at 21 years. The chief addition to the debate was from Deputy T.J. Fitzpatrick who argued in favour of reducing the age of majority to 18 years. The Second Stage was agreed to without a division.

On 11 July 1972 all the later stages of the Fourth Amendment were taken. No amendments to the Bill were passed and the Bill itself was passed without a division.

SEANAD ÉIREANN

On 13 July 1972, the Bill was introduced in the Seanad and passed the Second and subsequent stages. The debate was concerned with a whole range of subjects only loosely connected with the Bill. These included the general maturity of the over 18 year olds, their entitlement to marry, join the army or the Gardaí, to drink alcohol, to drive, to pay taxes and rates, etc., that it is good to bring them into politics, that there are more important changes to be made in the Constitution, and finally Article 44 and *Ne Temere*. Deputy Cunningham, the Parliamentary Secretary to the Minister for Local Government, accurately summed up the position in his opening remarks introducing the Bill:

> 'This House passed a resolution on 22 March last calling on the Taoiseach to take the steps necessary to allow all persons of 18 years and over the right to vote at all referenda and parliamentary and local elections. It is clear from this action and from the views expressed on all sides of this House on the recent Local Elections Bill that all parties are fully in favour of the principle of votes at 18. It is not necessary, therefore, for me at this stage to go into detail or to advance further arguments in favour of lowering the voting age.'

The flavour of the reception is given by the words of the opposition speaker Deputy Boland:

> 'This is a Bill which, as the Parliamentary Secretary has said, we can feel confident will be welcomed by all shades of opinion, both in this House and outside it.'

Senator Robinson, like some other speakers, expressed the desire to see further changes:

> 'The sort of change I should like to see and the matter I should like the people to be asked to vote on involves the removal of various elements of the 1937 Constitution which are divisive on religious and social grounds. I should like to refer briefly to a report of a

working-party set up by the Irish Theological Association which is reported in the June issue of *The Furrow* and which makes unanimous recommendations for changes in the Constitution.'

The Bill was put through Committee, reported without amendment, received for final consideration and passed without division.

Polling took place on 7 December 1972. As prescribed by the Referendum (Amendment) Act, 1972, the official polling card stated:

THE FOURTH AMENDMENT OF THE CONSTITUTION BILL, 1972, proposes to reduce the minimum voting age at Dáil and Presidential Elections and Referenda from 21 years to 18 years.

Total electorate		1,783,604
Total poll		903,439
Percentage poll		50.7%
Votes in favour	724,836	[84.6%]
Votes against	131,514	[15.4%]
Spoiled votes		47,089

The Bill was carried in all constituencies.
The Bill was signed by the President on 5 January 1973.

FOURTH AMENDMENT OF THE CONSTITUTION ACT, 1972

AN ACT TO AMEND THE CONSTITUTION
[*5 January 1973*]

WHEREAS by virtue of Article 46 of the Constitution any provision of the Constitution may be amended in the manner provided by that Article:

AND WHEREAS it is proposed to amend Article 16 of the Constitution:

BE IT THEREFORE ENACTED BY THE OIREACHTAS AS FOLLOWS:

1. Article 16 of the Constitution is hereby amended as follows:
    (*a*) 'ocht mbliadhna déag' shall be substituted for 'bliadhain agus fiche' in subsection 2° of section 1 of the Irish text,
    (*b*) 'eighteen years' shall be substituted for 'twenty-one years' in subsection 2° of section 1 of the English text.

2. (1) The amendment of the Constitution effected by this Act shall be called the Fourth Amendment of the Constitution.

    (2) This Act may be cited as the Fourth Amendment of the Constitution Act, 1972.

FIFTH AMENDMENT ACT — OIREACHTAS DEBATES

DÁIL ÉIREANN

The Fifth Amendment of the Constitution Bill, 1972, which removed the special position of the Catholic Church, and the recognition of other named religious denominations, from the *Bunreacht*, was introduced in the Dáil on 26 October 1972. The main themes of the debate were:

(a) everyone would prefer a total overhaul to piecemeal (sometimes described as timid) amendment of the Constitution, on the basis of proposals from an All-Party Committee;

(b) the Orange Order;

(c) Irish unity;

(d) the sectarianism of the southern state.

Deputy Cosgrave suggested that in view of the fact that the objectives of this Bill were not in dispute there might be some advantage in informally discussing the terms of the Bill before it was actually printed, which the Taoiseach said he would consider.

On 2 November 1972, the Second Stage was introduced by the Taoiseach Jack Lynch, who said:

> 'In the main, Article 44 of our Constitution is a charter for the free practice and profession of religion and in this respect I suggest that it is second to none in any part of the world.'

He went on to say:

> 'Whatever one may feel about the merits or otherwise of the two sub-sections of Article 44 now in question, there has been in recent years a growing feeling that the general provisions of Article 44 in regard to religious liberty are sufficient in themselves and that the specific listing of churches is neither desirable nor

necessary and should be deleted. It has been argued that this would contribute towards Irish unity or that the making of such a change would be an indication of the outward-looking approach of the Government and the people of Ireland in relation to unity. Whatever the force of these arguments may be, if these provisions are divisive in relation to the people living in Ireland, and they seem to be; if they are unnecessary, and this is now generally acknowledged then, in view of the firm guarantees of religious freedom and the freedom of conscience contained in the Constitution already, these two subsections ought to go.'

Fine Gael supported the Bill but Deputy Cosgrave declared:

'We would like to see a new Constitution. We look forward to the All-Party Committee recommending the necessary changes and providing the basis on which a new Constitution can be formulated.'

The Labour Party also supported the Bill but, as Deputy Cluskey stated:

'We do not think that the Constitution should be changed in the context of the Northern situation, we think it should be changed because it is right to change it.'

Some supporters of the Bill were at pains to assert that the Constitution as it stood was not tainted by sectarianism. Deputy Briscoe quoted from the welcome given to the Constitution in 1937 by the Dean of St Patrick's, Rev. D.F.R. Wilson and by the Senior Minister of the Adelaide Road Synagogue, Rev. A. Gudansky. The most curious contribution was from Deputy J. Lenehan who said:

'West of the Shannon the Constitution has never been thought about because it was always regarded as the 1937 Lenten Pastoral of Most Reverend John Charles McQuaid. It was held that his powers did not hold west of the Shannon and nobody took much notice of it.'

Many speakers emphasised, as did Deputy Ryan, that:

> 'It would be wrong to over-estimate the importance of this gesture in the North at present.'

On the other hand it was in fact intended as a gesture to the North. So it was certainly understood. Dr Cruise-O'Brien certainly took it thus:

> 'If this is an olive branch, and I suppose it is intended as one, it is being extended with a very languid hand, almost contemptuously. The implications of the Taoiseach's remarks . . . appear to be that any objections which are made to these subsections are unreasonable, silly, not well founded but that we are so magnanimous that we are prepared to drop these Articles even if the objections are unreasonable.'

Deputy R. Burke, in the most scholarly contribution to the debate, returned to de Valera's reasons for proposing the new Constitution in 1937. He argued that it had been strongly influenced by the Code of Social Principles which was published at Malines in 1929. Thus, he argued, Article 44 was not much more than an exposition of de Valera's view of church/state relations, which was provoked by pressure from **Maria Duce**. [**Maria Duce** was a Catholic group which at one time attracted thousands of people to its rallies and which, in the 1950s, campaigned for a Constitutional Amendment to declare the Catholic Church the one true church.] In support of his case he quoted Rev. Dr Newman in *Studies in Political Morality* (1962) and Mr Justice Gavan Duffy on the Tilson Case.[98] The Tilson case recognised the right of the mother to a full say in her children's education

---

98. (*In Re*) *Tilson*, (*Infants*) 1951 IR 1; 86 ILTR 49.

but it was widely interpreted as permitting the enforcement of *Ne Temere* agreements in the Civil Courts.

As for the Articles themselves, Deputy Desmond stated:

> 'It can only be described as a scandal to have given explicit *de facto* predominance to one religion within the whole island.'

Dr FitzGerald made one of the rare Dáil statements of the principles which should govern the framing of a constitution:

> 'Our Constitution should represent the common denominator of us all. It should protect those rights that are common to all, it should assert those principles that are common to all and it should not go beyond that.'

He also went on to combine two of the themes of the debate, domestic reform and the northern issue:

> 'I submit that in amending the Constitution we are motivated by several considerations one of which is the feeling that this is a first step towards creating the kind of society here that might bring unification nearer.'

The Second Stage was put and passed. The Committee and Final Stages were passed without amendment or division.

SEANAD ÉIREANN

All stages of the Fifth Amendment of the Constitution Bill, 1972 in the Seanad were taken on 3 November 1972. The debate ranged over many topics including a united Ireland, the Constitution itself, the Free Masons, the Tilson Case and divorce. The Bill was introduced by the Minister for Transport and Power, Deputy B. Lenihan, who said:

'Why, then, tackle now the amendment proposed in this Bill? . . . The reference in Article 44 of the Constitution to specific churches and in particular the special position of the Catholic Church, recognised in subsection (2) of section 1 of that Article, has been criticised as an obstacle to Irish unity.'

He was answered trenchantly by Deputy O'Higgins:

'I believe that the leaving out or leaving in of these sub-articles in Article 44 does not matter a rap in the context of national unity at present.'

Deputy O'Higgins went on to quote with approval an article by the Taoiseach in *Foreign Affairs* (July 1972) recommending a minimal Constitution for Ireland. Professor Kelly was not at all sure that the effort had been worthwhile:

'I find that after all the labouring of the mountain, after all the tastefully printed and distributed speeches of the Taoiseach over the last few years which talked about recognising other traditions and respecting them, after all the talk and acres of newsprint that have been expended on this apparent liberalisation of the Fianna Fail Party, we are confronted with this ridiculous little measure.'

Others, including Deputy Norton, were glad to be able to take the first, albeit small, step:

'We should have a secular Constitution in Ireland for the pluralist society which a united Ireland will contain. This amendment, as I have already said, is the first step in that direction and as such I should like to welcome it.'

The tenor of the Second Stage debate was conveyed by Senator Robinson:

'I regret so little is being done so late.'

The Bill was put through the Committee and Final Stages on the same day. On 7 November 1972, the Dáil received the following message from the Seanad: 'Seanad Éireann has passed the Fifth Amendment of the Constitution Bill, 1972, without amendment.'

Polling took place on 7 December 1972. As prescribed by the Referendum (Amendment) Act, 1972, the official polling card stated:

THE FIFTH AMENDMENT OF THE CONSTITUTION BILL, 1972, proposes to delete subsection 2° and 3° of Article 44.1 of the Constitution which provide as follows: [giving text of both paragraphs.]
If the proposal is approved Article 44 will provide as follows:
[giving text of whole Article as amended.]

Total electorate		1,783,604
Total poll		903,659
Percentage poll		50.7%
Votes in favour	721,003	[84.4%]
Votes against	133,430	[15.6%]
Spoiled votes		49,226

The Bill was carried in all constituencies.
The Bill was signed by the President on 5 January 1973.

FIFTH AMENDMENT OF THE CONSTITUTION ACT, 1972

AN ACT TO AMEND THE CONSTITUTION
[5 *January 1973*]

WHEREAS by virtue of Article 46 of the Constitution any provision of the Constitution may be amended in the manner provided by that Article:

AND WHEREAS it is proposed to amend Article 44 of the Constitution:

BE IT THEREFORE ENACTED BY THE OIREACHTAS AS FOLLOWS:

1. Article 44 of the Constitution is hereby amended as follows:
   (*a*) subsections 2° and 3° of section 1 of the Irish text shall be deleted,
   (*b*) subsections 2° and 3° of section 1 of the English text shall be deleted,
   (*c*) subsection 1° of section 1 of both texts shall be numbered as section 1.

2. (1) The amendment of the Constitution effected by this Act shall be called the Fifth Amendment of the Constitution.

   (2) This Act may be cited as the Fifth Amendment of the Constitution Act, 1972.

SIXTH AMENDMENT ACT — OIREACHTAS DEBATES

DÁIL ÉIREANN

On 13 December 1978, leave was granted to the Government under Taoiseach Charles J. Haughey to introduce in Dáil Éireann a Bill entitled an Act to amend the Constitution. The Second Stage of this, the Sixth Amendment of the Constitution (Adoption) Bill, 1978, was taken on 7 February 1979. The debate dealt with issues of adoption, the problem of interpreting the phrase 'first and paramount consideration' *vis-à-vis* the interest of the child, illegitimacy, that legislation should be more child-centred, the status of administrative decisions, Indemnity Acts and the Irish text. The Bill was introduced by the Minister for Justice, Deputy Gerry Collins:

> 'I move the Bill be now read a Second Time. The purpose of this Bill is to provide for a constitutional amendment which would ensure that adoption orders made by the Adoption Board cannot be declared to be invalid on the grounds that they were not made by a court . . . I think that technically it is a better provision than a similar one in the Private Members' Bill which was defeated here on 25 October . . . ever since the Supreme Court judgment [in *McL. v An Bórd Uchtála* in 1976] there appears to be no doubt that the opinion has been held in legal circles that if the court had had to deal in that case with the constitutional position they might have considered themselves obliged to find that, in making adoption orders, the Adoption Board were purporting to exercise powers of a kind that the Constitution reserves to the courts . . . There is no way, realistically, that we can offer to adopters an absolutely watertight guarantee that an adoption cannot be challenged. All we can seek to do is to create a situation in which the risk of a successful challenge is so small

that it would not in practice be a source of concern to the general body of adoptive parents, just as people who get married are not worried by the risk that a court may some day declare that a particular marriage was null and void . . . Words in the Constitution or a statute must be able to stand up to the scrutiny to which they are liable to be subjected in proceedings in the Courts and it is too late at that stage to say: "But that is not what I meant".'

The members of the Opposition were in agreement with the Bill. Deputy O'Keeffe said:

'Obviously we are aiming to ensure that the adoption procedure is constitutionally guaranteed. I am in total agreement with that aim.'

When the Second Stage resumed on 14 February 1979, Deputy O'Keeffe declared:

'If a single [legitimate] baby is forced out of this State because our laws do not permit it to be adopted here, surely we cannot just sit back in our comfortable chairs and let that position continue.'

Deputy Desmond, welcoming the Bill, made the expected reservation:

'This is a very narrow limited measure but in so far as it is necessary, we welcome it. The only criticisms we have is that it is not enough.'

A more serious legal point was raised by Deputy Kelly:

'What we are implicitly admitting here is that adoption is a non-limited function and that an adoption order cannot be made without exercising a function of a judicial nature. By admitting that, we may be implicitly pulling the ground from under some other

administrative function of which we are totally
unaware. That may be a very salutary result. I cannot
predict, I have not any idea; all I am saying is that we
are doing more here today than merely validating or
shoring up, or plugging a gap in an adoption system
which has been operating here for 27 years . . . The
other consequences of what we are doing here is that
it impliedly rules out, perhaps correctly — I think it is
right — Indemnity Acts . . . The point I am trying to
make is that by adopting this technique we implicitly,
tacitly are saying that ordinary Indemnity Acts are no
good, that they cannot be effective in this State from
now on, and that their purpose can only be achieved
via a solemn amendment to the constitution; I do not
think the Constitution allows Parliament arbitrarily to
take away people's rights of action in that way.'

The Second Stage was agreed without a division. The
Committee and Final Stages of the Bill were taken on 28
February 1979. Deputy O'Keeffe, who had expressed
reservations about the merit of making the child's welfare
paramount in law, had his proposed amendment to the Bill
declared out of order. For the Government Deputy Gerry
Collins stated:

'I am quite prepared to examine fully what the Deputy
says and if there is any way I can do anything about it
by the time of Committee Stage in the Seanad I will
have another look at it.'

The Bill passed all its stages without amendment. On 5 April
1979, the Dáil received the following message from the
Seanad: 'Seanad Éireann has passed the Sixth Amendment of
the Constitution (Adoption) Bill, 1978, without
amendment.'

SEANAD ÉIREANN

On 7 March 1979, the Second Stage of the Sixth Amendment of the Constitution Bill, 1978, was introduced in the Seanad by Minister for Justice, Deputy Gerry Collins who set out the purpose of the amendment:

> 'The purpose of this Bill is to ensure that adoption orders made by the Adoption Board cannot be declared to be invalid because they were not made by a court.'

Deputy Robinson, for the Opposition, stated that:

> 'the special problem in the McLaughlin case and in similar cases is that the parties, the natural mother and the natural father of the child, married and then they sought to have the adoption order set aside. Although in the decision of the Supreme Court the adoption order was struck down on procedural grounds — the mother was not sufficiently informed of her rights and did not give a full and free consent in the circumstances and the Supreme Court was critical of the procedure at that time — the basic issue is the potential clash between the inalienable and imprescriptible rights of the parents and the welfare and best interests of the child . . . The Minister has not given adoption orders the full security that they ought to have; he has met only half the problem that arose in the McLaughlin case and, above all, he has produced the most minimalist Bill on this question of adoption and the constitutionality of adoption orders that it was possible to devise. He has left out of the picture all the other problems and needs of children which are so important and worthy of attention in this International Year of the Child.'

The Seanad Second Stage passed.

On 28 March 1979 the Seanad Committee Stage was taken and passed without amendment.

On 5 April 1978 the Seanad Report and Final Stage was taken. Senator Keating moved an amendment on behalf of Senator Robinson intended to permit the adoption of legitimate children:

> 'I move amendment No. 1: . . . In page 4, line 36, after "person" to insert "notwithstanding the status of such person".'

Senator Alexis FitzGerald:

> 'I support the amendment [above] which has been tabled in Senator Robinson's and my name.'

For the Government, Senator E. Ryan declared:

> 'I disagree with Senator FitzGerald on the desirability of having the power to adopt legitimate children.'

He was supported by the Minister of State at the Department of Justice, Deputy Andrews:

> 'The Government are simply not prepared to open up adoption to legitimate children.'

Senator Robinson replied:

> 'I do not know of any other country that prohibits the possibility of adoption for legitimate children. If the Minister is aware of other countries perhaps he would enlighten us about them. It is an accidental legal technicality and since it is a legal technicality surely we should address our minds to removing that technicality so that we can decide on whether or not we could introduce legislation.'

The amendment was put and declared lost.

The Bill was received for final consideration and passed. The referendum took place on 5 July 1979. As prescribed by the Referendum (Amendment) Act, 1979, the polling card contained the following statement:

THE SIXTH AMENDMENT OF THE CONSTITUTION (ADOPTION) BILL, 1978, proposes that an adoption which is in accordance with laws enacted by the Oireachtas shall not be invalid solely by reason of the fact that the relevant order or authorisation was not made or given by a judge or court but by a person or body designated for the purpose by those laws. The Bill relates to past as well as future adoptions. Its object is to ensure that adoption orders made by An Bórd Uchtála (The Adoption Board) will not be in danger of being declared to be invalid because they were not made in a court.

Total electorate		2,179,466
Total poll		623,476
Percentage poll		28.6%
Votes in favour	601,694	[98.97%]
Votes against	6,265	[1.03%]
Spoiled votes		15,517

The Bill was carried in all constituencies.
The Bill was signed by the President on 3 August 1979.

SIXTH AMENDMENT OF THE CONSTITUTION (ADOPTION) ACT, 1979

AN ACT TO AMEND THE CONSTITUTION
[*3 August 1979*]

WHEREAS by virtue of Article 46 of the Constitution any provision of the Constitution may be amended in the manner provided by that Article:

AND WHEREAS it is proposed to amend Article 37 of the Constitution:

BE IT THEREFORE ENACTED BY THE OIREACHTAS AS FOLLOWS:

1. Article 37 of the Constitution is hereby amended as follows:
    (*a*) the section set out in Part I of the Schedule to this Act shall be added to the Irish text,
    (*b*) the section set out in Part II of the Schedule to this Act shall be added to the English text,
    (*c*) Article 37 of both texts shall be numbered as section 1 of that Article.

2. (1) The amendment of the Constitution effected by this Act shall be called the Sixth Amendment of the Constitution.

    (2) This Act may be cited as the Sixth Amendment of the Constitution (Adoption) Act, 1979.

SCHEDULE
Part II

2. No adoption of a person taking effect or expressed to take effect at any time after the coming into operation of this Constitution under laws enacted by the Oireachtas and being an adoption pursuant to an order made or an authorisation given by any person or body of persons designated by those laws to exercise such functions and powers was or shall be invalid by reason only of the fact that such persons or body of persons was not a judge or a court appointed or established as such under this Constitution.

SEVENTH AMENDMENT ACT — OIREACHTAS DEBATES

DÁIL ÉIREANN

The Seventh Amendment of the Constitution (Election of Members of Seanad Éireann by Institutions of Higher Education) Bill, 1979, was introduced by the Government under Taoiseach Charles J. Haughey in Dáil Éireann on 3 May 1979. When the Second Stage was introduced on 22 May 1979, it was moved by the Minister for Education, Deputy John Wilson:

> 'I move that the Bill be now read a Second Time. The purpose of this Bill is to remove an obstacle in the way of legislation to deal with university reorganisation.'

In his remarks he spoke particularly of the dissolution of the NUI which was the only university he mentioned. The position of Trinity College was raised by an Opposition speaker, Deputy Hogan:

> 'I would argue that if the individual representation of Trinity is to be removed—we have no indication yet whether it is or not—could the Minister give us some indication of his further intentions in this regard?'

Deputy Kelly spoke at length on the nature and structure of the Seanad saying that he would allow senators to be elected by graduates of all the institutions of higher education, but he considered the amendment messy. He also raised a wider issue:

> 'By going out of our way in Article 18 to make it clear that an element mentioned in the Constitution is not protected from abolition, namely the universities, you are inviting the implication that other things mentioned in the Constitution are protected from abolition, such

as a census or a jury or the name of the city of Dublin. Of course I am all in favour of entrenching juries against abolition but we should know what we are doing here.'

The Bill passed the Second Stage without a division. The Committee and Final Stages were all taken on 23 May 1979. After a brief debate in which a couple of amendments to the Bill were proposed and withdrawn, the Bill passed without amendment and without division.

SEANAD ÉIREANN

The Bill was introduced in Seanad Éireann on 31 May 1979. The Minister for Education, Deputy Wilson, more or less reiterated what he had told the Dáil, that the purpose of the Bill was to facilitate, at some time in the future, the dissolution of the National University of Ireland and the establishment of independent universities at Dublin, Cork and Galway, and the determination of the future status of St Patrick's College, Maynooth, the colleges of education in Drumcondra, Blackrock and Limerick, and the College of Surgeons. Senator Robinson welcomed the retention of university Senators, enumerated the benefits of having them, spoke of their useful and constructive role, their independent initiative and voice over the years and the importance of their contact with Northern Ireland, especially in the case of Dublin University Senators. Dr West provided an extremely useful potted history of university representation in Ireland from very early times. Professor Murphy declared:

'One welcomes this Bill if only in the first place because it means that the legislation for reforming university structures is imminent . . . The National University of Ireland in particular has been under sentence of death for so long now—and the odour of mortality is palpable in Merrion Square—that it is time, in all decency, to administer the *coup de grâce.*'

Senator Hussey attempted to widen the debate:

> 'We should have an opportunity to get down to real
> debate about the Constitution instead of stop-gap
> amendments which clear up some little point which
> obstructs some other piece of legislation. We really
> should be considering the Constitution itself. I am
> going to take this opportunity, since we are amending
> an Article of the Constitution, to discuss other
> amendments of that Article that we are amending . . . I
> should like to see the number of seats to be elected by
> graduates of universities and other institutes of
> education dramatically increased and I would also like
> to support the view that we must, if at all possible,
> attract Northern Ireland people to interest themselves
> in the second House of the Oireachtas . . . I am
> suggesting that we go further in this Bill than the
> minimal amendments to Article 18 as it appears before
> us and that we should amend other sections of the
> article, notably sections 3 and 4 in order to create 17
> seats to be distributed among the third-level institutions
> of the whole island. [The seventeen to be made up of
> the existing university six plus the Taoiseach's eleven.]'

A quite different position was adopted by Senator Keating:

> 'Let me use this opportunity to say that I persist in
> thinking it is a dreadful Constitution, a hindrance to the
> development of this country and that we ought to have
> a new one and not be doing it piecemeal . . . I have
> difficulty in approving of the idea of university seats at
> all, but as Bernard Shaw said to the man who was
> booing, "who am I among so many?"'

He went on to say:

> 'I think there ought to be proportionality in the
> allocation of seats between institutions . . . I want to see
> some regionality west of the Shannon . . .'

He also discussed the nature of Irish higher education and its bias against the sciences and technology. The Bill was reported without amendment, received for final consideration and passed.

The referendum took place on 5 July 1979. As prescribed by the Referendum (Amendment) Act, 1979, the polling card contained the following statement:

THE SEVENTH AMENDMENT OF THE CONSTITUTION (ELECTION OF MEMBERS OF SEANAD ÉIREANN BY INSTITUTIONS OF HIGHER EDUCATION) BILL, 1979, proposes the election by universities and other institutions of higher education specified by law of such number of members of Seanad Éireann, not exceeding 6, as may be specified by law. Those so elected would be in substitution for an equal number of the members elected at present (3 each) by the National University of Ireland and the University of Dublin. The Bill also proposes that nothing in Article 18 of the Constitution shall prohibit the dissolution by law of those Universities.

Total electorate		2,179,466
Total poll		622,646
Percentage poll		28.6%
Votes in favour	552,600	[92.4%]
Votes against	45,484	[7.6%]
Spoiled votes		24,562

The Bill was carried in all constituencies.
The Bill was signed by the President on 3 August 1979.

SEVENTH AMENDMENT OF THE CONSTITUTION (ELECTION OF MEMBERS OF SEANAD ÉIREANN BY INSTITUTIONS OF HIGHER EDUCATION) ACT, 1979

AN ACT TO AMEND THE CONSTITUTION
[*3 August 1979*]

WHEREAS by virtue of Article 46 of the Constitution any provision of the Constitution may be amended in the manner provided by that Article:

AND WHEREAS it is proposed to amend Article 18 of the Constitution:

BE IT THEREFORE ENACTED BY THE OIREACHTAS AS FOLLOWS:

1. Article 18 of the Constitution is hereby amended as follows:
   (*a*) the subsections set out in *Part I* of the Schedule to this Act shall be added to section 4 of the Irish text,
   (*b*) the subsections set out in *Part II* of the Schedule to this Act shall be added to section 4 of the English text,
   (*c*) section 4 of both texts shall be numbered as section 4.1°.

2. (1) The amendment of the Constitution effected by this Act shall be called the Seventh Amendment of the Constitution.

   (2) This Act may be cited as the Seventh Amendment of the Constitution (Election of Members of Seanad Éireann by Institutions of Higher Education) Act, 1979.

SCHEDULE
Part II

2° Provision may be made by law for the election, on a franchise and in the manner to be provided by law, by one or more of the following institutions, namely:

  i.   the universities mentioned in subsection 1° of this section,
  ii. any other institutions of higher education in the State,

of so many members of Seanad Éireann as may be fixed by law in substitution for an equal number of the members to be elected pursuant to paragraphs i and ii of the said subsection 1°.

A member or members of Seanad Éireann may be elected under this subsection by institutions grouped together or by a single institution.

3° Nothing in this Article shall be invoked to prohibit the dissolution by law of a university mentioned in subsection 1° of this section.

EIGHTH AMENDMENT ACT — OIREACHTAS DEBATES

DÁIL ÉIREANN

The Eighth Amendment of the Constitution Bill, 1982, proposing to recognise the right to life of the unborn, was first introduced by the Government under Taoiseach Charles J. Haughey in Dáil Éireann in 1982. It lapsed on the dissolution of the 23rd Dáil and following a general election was restored to the Order Paper by the Government under Taoiseach Garret FitzGerald on 2 February 1983. In the subsequent Oireachtas debates there was considerable heat. The debate was very long with many Deputies speaking. There was much repetition as many speakers were concerned with putting their position on record and expressing their support for the arguments of one side or the other, rather than offering new arguments. No one spoke in favour of making abortion legal. Those opposing the Amendment spoke against the necessity of having such an Article in the Constitution. The debate was interesting in that the Government was less in favour of the Bill than the Opposition. There was also a claim that the amendment was sectarian, and that the campaign outside the Oireachtas was very bitter. For much of the debate it was uncertain whether the Government would continue with the same words or change them, and this led to confusion as to whether a reference in the debate to an 'amendment' was a reference to the Bill or to a proposed amendment to the Bill. There was also a question raised on 27 April 1983 as to the status of pre-1937 legislation in relation to the amendment.

The Second Stage was introduced by the Minister for Justice, Deputy Noonan on 9 February 1983:

'The Bill proposes to amend section 3 of Article 40 of the Constitution by adding the following subsection—

"3° The State acknowledges the right to life of the
unborn and, with due regard to the equal right to life
of the mother, guarantees in its laws to respect, and,
as far as practicable, by its laws to defend and
vindicate that right."'

He continued:

'It has become apparent that judicial decisions
concerning abortion can alter fundamentally what had
been accepted to be the law, even to the extent of
introducing what is virtually a system of abortion on
demand . . . Recent developments in cases taken under
the European Convention on Human Rights are such as
to suggest that the Convention may be interpreted as
conferring a right to have an abortion . . . on the one
hand, I have been advised that, on one particular
interpretation, the amendment could in fact have an
effect very different indeed from what it might at first
sight appear to have and that it could positively
facilitate the introduction of abortion on a very wide
scale . . . On the other hand, on another interpretation
of the text, which has been put to me by a very
responsible authority as a probable interpretation, it
could require the State to make the 1861 Act more
restrictive than it is, which I think is something that
nobody has suggested is either necessary or
appropriate . . . In commending the motion to the
House—the motion that the Bill be now read a second
time—I do so on the basis of what I have said earlier,
namely, that in approving of the principle of the Bill,
which is what the House does in giving a Bill a second
reading, Deputies would not as far as I am concerned
be committing themselves to the particular wording
now proposed or any other particular form of wording
but only to the principle which I think we all

understand. On that basis I recommend the Bill to the House.'

The Second Stage resumed on 17 February 1983. Dr O'Hanlon, for the Opposition, stated:

'Fianna Fáil believe the wording we put forward is correct and nothing that has been said has convinced us that we should alter that view.'

For the Labour Party, which was a party in the coalition Government, Deputy B. Desmond stated:

'I would go so far as to say that for the future the present ban on abortion may be argued to be put at greater risk through adoption of this form of words or any similar form than by leaving the whole question to the normal process of statutory control.'

This point was taken up in more detail by Deputy Shatter:

'The irony is that I have no doubt, not merely from the interpretation the Attorney General has given but from the other interpretations that can be validly taken from the amendment, that if it in its present form becomes part of our Constitution it will essentially secure a constitutional judgment in the not too distant future requiring the House to enact legislation to permit women to have abortions . . . There is not a Member of this House who can categorically state that if this matter were dealt with before our courts this year, next year, or in 20 years time, one of these interpretations to permit, and indeed constitutionally require, abortion would not be accepted.'

He concluded:

'That there is a variety of valid, different interpretations of this Article means that it is not appropriate to be included in the Constitution to carry out the intent of those who believe that such an Article is required.'

When the Second Stage resumed on 23 February 1983, the Opposition supported the Bill as it stood. Deputy Flynn said:

> 'The insertion of this amendment in the Constitution will mean simply that abortion cannot and will not be made legal either through legislation or judicial decision.'

This confidence led to suspicion of those who opposed the Bill. On 2 March 1983, when the Second Stage resumed once again, Deputy Flynn stated:

> 'The anti-amendment campaign, as it is working its way through the system, is no more and no less than—in fact, virtually the same as—the pro-abortion lobby.'

On 8 March 1983, still on the Second Stage, Deputy O'Dea replied:

> 'If Deputy Shatter's argument is taken then, in effect, we should abandon the entire Constitution as it now stands because many things may be found in the future to be implicit in the Constitution as it now stands which are not foreseen at the moment.'

When the Second Stage again resumed on 24 March 1983, it emerged that the Government was considering an alternative clause. In response the leader of the Opposition Deputy Haughey stated:

> 'The wording in the Bill states:
> "3° The State acknowledges the right to life of the unborn and, with due regard to the equal right to life of the mother, guarantees in its laws to respect, and, as far as practicable, by its laws to defend and vindicate that right."
> That is a very clear and positive pro-life amendment.

The wording now being suggested to us by the Government and the Taoiseach is:
"Nothing in this Constitution shall be invoked to invalidate any provision of a law on the ground that it prohibits abortion".
As far as we are concerned that it totally unacceptable because it is entirely negative. It is not pro-life.'

The Second Stage was put to a vote and the question was declared carried by 140 votes to 11.

The Committee Stage was introduced on 27 April 1983. Deputy Noonan introduced the amendment to the Bill quoted above:

'Briefly, those defects [sic] are twofold: first, that the expression "the unborn" is very ambiguous; second, that the reference to the equal rights of the mother is insufficient to guarantee that operations necessary to save the live of the mother but resulting in the death of the foetus may continue . . . Now, the position in which we find ourselves is that I [as Minister] am sponsoring this amendment and, in effect, the Opposition are sponsoring the existing wording.'

Dr Woods, for the Opposition, outlined their position and concluded:

'Therefore, we regard the wording which we have in our amendment as satisfactory.'

The amendment to the Bill was put to a vote and declared lost by 65 votes to 87. The Bill, unamended, was then put to a vote and declared carried by 85 votes to 11.

SEANAD ÉIREANN

On 4 May 1983, the Eighth Amendment of the Constitution Bill, 1982, Second Stage was introduced in the Seanad. For once the question of possible differences in meanings between the Irish and English texts seemed important, but it was teased out on individual matters and the issue, as such, of the status of the Irish text was not debated.

The Bill was introduced in an extremely short speech by the Minister for Justice, Deputy Noonan:

> 'When close examination of the text revealed defects, an alternative text was approved by a majority of our Parliamentary Party but it did not secure acceptance in the Dáil. The Dáil has made its decision and it is now a matter for this House to consider its attitude.'

Senator Robinson replied in a very long speech:

> 'I move amendment No. 1: To delete all words after "That" and substitute the following: "Seanad Éireann declines to give a second reading to the Eighth Amendment of the Constitution Bill, 1982, on the grounds that the Bill is so unclear and ambiguous that it is not the proper subject for a proposal to be submitted to the people in a referendum." . . . The duty, then, on each of us in this House is to ask ourselves if this proposal is a fair and reasonable proposal to submit by way of referendum to the people . . . The problem, therefore, is that the various words and phrases in the amendment can have completely opposite meanings . . . it is so unclear and so ambiguous that it has been criticised severely and in an unprecedented way by the two chief law officers of the State, the Attorney General and the Director of Public Prosecutions.'

In support of the Bill, Senator Lanigan replied:

> 'Although there is sometimes ambiguity in Bills brought before Parliament, there is not much ambiguity in the Bill before us.'

Senator Hanafin argued in favour of the Bill on its merits but without reference to the content of Senator Robinson's contribution:

> 'We who have put forward the amendment that is now the Dáil amendment want to put into the Constitution the right to life of the unborn child so that any consideration of introducing abortion here in the future would have to involve putting the matter before the people.'

On 5 May 1983 the Second Stage resumed with Senator E. Ryan:

> 'An amendment was put down in this House saying that the Bill should not be passed on the grounds that it is unclear and ambiguous and is not a proper subject to be submitted to the people in a referendum. If one looks at the amendment proposed it is divided, roughly speaking, into three different sentences. The first part of it says the State acknowledges the right to life of the unborn and that is a perfectly clear statement of principle. There is nothing uncertain or vague about that . . . It has been suggested that the word "unborn" is uncertain because it is not followed by "unborn child". This is a very pedantic point which really does not stand up to consideration. There are already in the Constitution a number of similar words used in Article 45.4.1°. There is reference to the "aged" and "infirm". The same pedants would argue that it should be the "aged person" and the "infirm person" . . . If one looks at the remainder of the proposed amendment to the Constitution it says "guarantees in its laws to respect and as far as is practicable by its laws to defend and vindicate that right". That exact same sentence is already in the Constitution Article 40.3 . . . To say that this wording is unclear or ambiguous does not stand up to examination . . . The Supreme Court, far from resenting or feeling that their rights are being infringed

upon, will be very happy to have the Constitution amended and clarified in this way.

Reference has been made to opinions expressed by the Attorney General and the DPP. I have the greatest respect for the Attorney General and the DPP and for their opinions. But they are merely opinions. I find it impossible to agree with their views as to the likely effect the amendment would have on the ordinary [sic] law from a practical point of view. I cannot see the Supreme Court deciding in any different way in relation to this question than they would at present.'

The Second Stage continued until 11 May 1983, when it was carried. On 18 May 1983 the Committee Stage began during which Senator Ross proposed to amend the Bill in the same way as the Minister for Justice had proposed in the Dáil. In this he was not supported by Deputy Noonan who said:

'The only practical effect the adoption of this amendment would have would be to delay the passage of the Bill and the holding of the referendum. In my view that would not be in the public interest. Accordingly, I cannot recommend the amendment.'

Senator O'Leary declared:

'The view that there is something objectionable to tying the hands of the Legislature is wrong. I think there is nothing objectionable to tying the hands of the Legislature in this or any other matter. Those who deny the right to tie the hands of the Legislature fail to recognise that we live not just in a democracy but in a constitutional democracy. They have failed to appreciate that our type of democracy is fundamentally different from that of our ancestors. They are, if I might say so, in the tradition of the Irish Parliamentary Party, not in the tradition of the Irish Republic. They believe and what they are really saying is that Legislatures should not be tied, they should be capable of passing and free to pass laws as and when they think fit in a manner similar to the power and freedom which the Houses of Parliament of the United Kingdom have. They fail to recognise that ours is a constitutional democracy which is moulded more on the style of the United States of America, where there are fundamental rights which no State or federal legislature has a right to overrule. What is wrong is that people have failed to recognise the transition we made by the adoption of the Constitution in 1937, and they are not yet accepting the fact that we are no longer in a parliamentary democracy, but in a constitutional parliamentary democracy. There is a fundamental difference . . . There is no difficulty or problem when you are talking about the infirm or the aged in recognising and acknowledging that you are talking about human beings. The problem when you are talking about the unborn is of a fundamentally different character because the whole problem is that, even the addition of the word "child" as suggested by Senator O'Donoghue does not solve the problem . . . The whole question of what you mean by a child must be defined because, of course, it is not a child in the ordinary accepted sense of the word; it is a child before birth.'

On 19 May 1983 the Committee Stage resumed and the Bill passed without amendment.

On 25 May 1983 the Seanad Report Stage commenced. Senator McGuinness[99] proposed an amendment to the Bill after 'unborn' to insert 'which shall not include the fertilised ovum prior to the time at which such fertilised ovum becomes implanted in the wall of the uterus'. This proposal was strongly supported by Senator Robinson and Senator

---

99. Catherine McGuinness: Senior Counsel; Member of Seanad Éireann, 1979-87; Member of the Counsel of State, 1988-91; appointed Circuit Court Judge on 28 February, 1994.

Michael D. Higgins. The Minister for State at the Department of Labour, Deputy G. Birmingham, replied:

> 'Realistically, I cannot see that this amendment would have any chance of being accepted by the Dáil. It could result only in further delaying the Bill and this would not be in the public interest. In the circumstances I am not in a position to recommend acceptance of the amendment.'

Senator McGuinness stated:

> 'I suggest, and I have as good an authority as Fr Fergal O'Connor of Ally to back me up, that far more people consider abortion as an acceptable alternative since this debate started than ever would have beforehand.'

Senator McGuinness's amendment was lost by 10 votes to 18. Senator Robinson declared:

> 'One can talk about GUBU and unprecedented situations but this is the first time in my parliamentary experience that the Taoiseach, the Minister for Justice and the Minister of State with responsibility for women's affairs have said on the record that a particular measure is potentially dangerous to the life of pregnant women; not to their economic outlook, to their social standing or to their job prospects, but to their lives and yet they are not going to use the measures available to them as a Government to prevent this particular formulation from going forward to the people in a referendum.'

On 26 May 1983 the Report Stage resumed and the Final Stage was taken. Senator McGuinness proposed to delete 'equal' and substitute 'prior' but the proposal lost by 15 votes to 8. The proposal to proceed to the Fifth Stage passed without division. Senator Robinson made a last argument:

> 'The basic flaw in this amendment is that it is so uncertain in its scope and so potentially contradictory in its meaning and so potentially damaging to existing practices in the area of family planning and medical treatment . . . '

The question was put and declared carried by 14 votes to 6.

Polling took place on 7 September 1983. As prescribed by the Referendum (Amendment) Act, 1983, the polling card stated:

THE EIGHTH AMENDMENT OF THE CONSTITUTION BILL, 1982, proposes to add the subsection here following to Article 40.3 of the Constitution: [as per Schedule].

Total electorate		2,358,651
Total poll		1,265,994
Percentage poll		53.7%
Votes in favour	841,233	[67%]
Votes against	416,136	[33%]
Spoiled votes		8,625

The Bill was carried in all but five of the forty-one constituencies.

The Bill was signed by the President on 7 October 1983.

EIGHTH AMENDMENT OF THE CONSTITUTION ACT, 1983

AN ACT TO AMEND THE CONSTITUTION
[*7 October 1983*]

WHEREAS by virtue of Article 46 of the Constitution any provision of the Constitution may be amended in the manner provided by that Article:

AND WHEREAS it is proposed to amend Article 40 of the Constitution:

BE IT THEREFORE ENACTED BY THE OIREACHTAS AS FOLLOWS:

1. Article 40 of the Constitution is hereby amended as follows:
   (*a*) the subsection set out in *Part I* of the Schedule to this Act shall be added to section 3 of the Irish text,
   (*b*) the subsection set out in *Part II* of the Schedule to this Act shall be added to section 3 of the English text.

2. (1) The amendment of the Constitution effected by this Act shall be called the Eighth Amendment of the Constitution.

   (2) This Act may be cited as the Eighth Amendment of the Constitution Act, 1983.

SCHEDULE
Part II

3° The State acknowledges the right to life of the unborn and, with due regard to the equal right to life of the mother, guarantees in its laws to respect, and, as far as practicable, by its laws to defend and vindicate that right.

NINTH AMENDMENT ACT — OIREACHTAS DEBATES

DÁIL ÉIREANN

On 5 April 1984 the Ninth Amendment of the Constitution Bill, 1984, proposing to give votes to non-Irish nationals, was introduced in Dáil Éireann by the Government under Taoiseach Garret FitzGerald. It arose from an earlier Bill which had been referred to the Supreme Court by the President.

The Second Stage was introduced on 11 April 1984, by the Minister for the Environment, Deputy Kavanagh:

'I move: That the Bill be now read a Second Time. The purpose of the Bill is to enable the people to decide in a referendum whether the Constitution should be amended to enable the right to vote at Dáil elections to be extended to persons other than citizens by legislation enacted by the Oireachtas . . . The principle of extending the right to vote at Dáil elections to persons other than Irish citizens has already been endorsed by the House in approving the Electoral (Amendment) Bill, 1983. That measure applied only to British citizens.'

For the Opposition, Deputy Molloy declared:

'Fianna Fáil will support the proposal to amend the Constitution to give power to the Oireachtas to extend the right to vote in Dáil elections to persons ordinarily resident in the country but who are not Irish citizens.'

The Second Stage was put and agreed to without a division. The Committee and Final Stages were taken on the same day. The Bill passed all stages without amendment.

SEANAD ÉIREANN

The Bill was introduced in Seanad Éireann on 11 April 1984. By and large it was welcomed by all. The concerns most expressed were that disabled Irish citizens could not have a postal vote and that the right to vote in Irish elections should be similarly extended to other EEC nationals. The Minister of State at the Department of the Environment Deputy F. O'Brien, introducing the Bill, said much the same as had been said when the Bill was being introduced in the Dáil:

'The purpose of the Bill is to enable the people to decide in a referendum whether the Constitution should be amended to enable the right to vote at Dáil elections to be extended to persons other than citizens by legislation enacted the the Oireachtas . . . The amendment to the Constitution proposed in the Bill does not extend to granting voting rights to non-citizens at Presidential elections and referenda. The import of the advice available following the Supreme Court decision on the Electoral (Amendment) Bill, 1983, is that the basic concept of a Constitution is that of a fundamental law given by citizens to themselves. To give non-citizens the right in the Constitution to change the fundamental law enshrined in it would be contrary to this basic concept . . . With regard to the question of a Presidential election, the President holds a special position under the Constitution as Head of State. He takes precedence over all other persons in the State and, in a special way, is the direct representative of the Irish people. Having regard to the nature of his office and his role under the Constitution, it would seem inappropriate that he should be elected by anybody other than citizens of this country, and indeed the weight of opinion following the Supreme Court decision bears this out . . . If the Bill is approved by the people on 14 June the provisional certificate showing the result of the referenda will be published in *Iris*

Oifigiúil and, if not contested, will become final after 21 days. The Bill will then be signed by the President towards the middle of July.'

The Second Stage was put and agreed to without a division. The Bill was reported without amendment, received for final consideration and passed without division.

Polling took place on 14 June 1984 (on the same day as the European Parliamentary election). As prescribed by the Referendum (Amendment) Act, 1984, the polling card stated:

THE NINTH AMENDMENT OF THE CONSTITUTION BILL, 1984, proposes to extend the right conferred on citizens to vote at elections for members of Dáil Éireann to such other persons in the State who have reached the age of 18 years as may be specified by legislation enacted by the Oireachtas.

Total electorate		2,399,257
Total poll		1,138,895
Percentage poll		47.5%
Votes in favour	828,483	[75.4%]
Votes against	270,250	[24.6%]
Spoiled votes		40,162

The Bill was carried in every county and county borough [which were deemed to be constituencies for the purpose of the referendum under section 2 of the Referendum (Amendment) Act, 1984].

The Bill was signed by the President on 2 August 1984.

NINTH AMENDMENT OF THE CONSTITUTION ACT, 1984

AN ACT TO AMEND THE CONSTITUTION
[*2 August 1984*]

WHEREAS by virtue of Article 46 of the Constitution any provision of the Constitution may be amended in the manner provided by that Article:

AND WHEREAS it is proposed to amend Article 16 of the Constitution:

BE IT THEREFORE ENACTED BY THE OIREACHTAS AS FOLLOWS:

1. Article 16 of the Constitution is hereby amended as follows:
    (*a*) the subsection set out in *Part I* of the Schedule to this Act shall be substituted for subsection 2° of section 1 of the Irish text,
    (*b*) the subsection set out in *Part II* of the Schedule to this Act shall be substituted for subsection 2° of section 1 of the English text,
    (*c*) 'a dhícháileochadh saoránach ar bith nó duine ar bith eile, ar an bhforas céanna sin,' shall be inserted after 'de Dháil Éireann nó' in subsection 3° of section 1 of the Irish text.
    (*d*) 'or other person' shall be inserted after 'disqualifying any citizen' in subsection 3° of section 1 of the English text.

2. (1) The amendment of the Constitution effected by this Act shall be called the Ninth Amendment of the Constitution.

(2) This Act may be cited as the Ninth Amendment of the Constitution Act, 1984.

SCHEDULE
Part II

2° i. All citizens, and

ii. such other persons in the State as may be determined by law,

without distinction of sex who have reached the age of eighteen years who are not disqualified by law and comply with the provisions of the law relating to the election of members of Dáil Éireann, shall have the right to vote at an election for members of Dáil Éireann.

TENTH AMENDMENT ACT — OIREACHTAS DEBATES

DÁIL ÉIREANN

The Tenth Amendment of the Constitution Bill, 1987, proposing to permit ratification of the Single European Act, was introduced in the Dáil by the Government under Taoiseach Charles J. Haughey on 22 April 1987. It arose after Mr Raymond Crotty took the issue to the Supreme Court which held that the matter should be put to the people in a Constitutional Referendum. The debate concerned the merits of membership of the EEC, fears for our neutrality, the effect of the Supreme Court decision on earlier international treaties, the merits of a wider amendment to place future and existing treaties out of danger and the right of the Supreme Court to supervise the Executive in carrying out foreign policy. The Bill was generally supported but it was opposed by the Workers Party on economic and political grounds. Introducing the motion 'that the Bill be now read a second time', the Taoiseach said:

> 'the [Supreme] Court declared, by a separate majority decision, that ratification of the Single [European] Act, in so far as it contains Title III, is impermissible under the Constitution and that it could only be ratified if an appropriate constitutional amendment were made . . . It must be accepted, however, that the judgments [of the Supreme Court] in so far as they affect the boundaries between executive and judicial areas of responsibility have caused widespread surprise.'

That surprise was due, to some extent, to the acceptance of the assurance by de Valera, in the Dáil on 11 May 1937, that under the new Constitution the Government would be responsible for foreign affairs. The Taoiseach went on to discuss the merits of the Single European Act:

'Our future is crucially linked and dependent on a Community which is growing and developing and is committed to ensuring that the benefits of further progress are shared by all the Community's regions. I am convinced that the great majority of the Irish people want Ireland to continue as an active, committed member of that Community and I accordingly commend the Bill to the House.'

An apparent difficulty of the Bill being too narrow was raised by Deputy D. O'Malley who said:

'if, this week, we include only the Single European Act in the proposed constitutional amendment there will be a presumption that we did not wish to cure the constitutional infirmities that seem to affect the ratification of so many other treaties and agreements, including the Anglo-Irish Agreement.'

Deputy McDowell, claiming the support of Hogan and Morgan's *Administrative Law*, added:

'Put succinctly, because we had an option as to how we would enact European directives as part of our domestic law, because we exercise that option in a particular way and because it is one which falls foul of Article 15.2 of the Constitution, it follows that many of our regulations made under the 1973 Act are constitutionally infirm as things stand.'

He went on to point out that the Bill also failed to deal with the European Patent Convention signed in December 1989.

On 23 April 1987 the Second Stage resumed, the question was put and the House divided: Tá, 108; Níl 29. The Second Stage was declared carried.

The Committee and Final Stages were taken together, along with the Referendum (Amendment) Bill, on 24 April 1987 with An Ceann Comhairle declaring:

> 'As it is now 4 o'clock I am required to put the following question in accordance with the resolution of the Dáil of 22 April and the order of the House today. The question is that the Tenth Amendment of the Constitution Bill, 1987, is hereby agreed to in Committee and is reported to the House without amendment and Fourth Stage is hereby completed and the Bill is hereby passed, and that the referendum (Amendment) Bill, 1987, is hereby agreed to in Committee and is reported to the House without amendment and Fourth Stage is hereby completed and the Bill is hereby passed.'

The question was put to the House and the Dáil divided: Tá, 123; Níl, 17. Accordingly the question was declared carried.

SEANAD ÉIREANN

The Bill was introduced on 25 April 1987. The Single European Act was welcomed from both sides of the House. The themes in the debate included our neutrality and sovereignty but much of it was in fact a re-run of the debate on the Single European Act of the previous December. The Government did give an undertaking 'to give serious consideration to the conduct of international relations which, under Article 29, resides with the democratically elected government, subject to the approval of the Dáil'. Introducing the Bill the Minister for Foreign Affairs, Deputy Lenihan, said:

> 'This debate is a stage in a process which will enable the Irish people, on 26 May, to exercise their sovereign right under the Constitution to decide whether the State may ratify the Single European Act . . . The

Government agree that larger issues concerning the State's power to conduct its foreign policy have been thrown up by the Supreme Court ruling . . . Of their nature, these issues require very careful and in-depth consideration and quite clearly, our objective in relation to the Single European Act, that is to say, its speedy ratification, does not allow for the attention that should be devoted to the wider issue . . . The constraints on our sovereignty represented by the Single European Act are of a piece with the constraint we accepted and in [sic] incorporated in the Constitution when we joined the Community in 1973.'

In reply Senator Manning said:

'I think we have every right to say—and we will not be seen as being in any way disrespectful—that the arguments about constitutionality appear to be unconvincing and indeed off-centre, that the import of the judgment is to shift from the Oireachtas and the Government of the day the right to make foreign policy, and in so doing bring about a situation which the framer and the founder of our Constitution, Eamon de Valera, certainly never envisaged, and something which surprises and dismays many independent constitutional lawyers in the wider community. But given a written Constitution, given the existence of a judicial review, it was inevitable that a judgment of this sort would appear on some issue at some time.'

Senator Fennell expressed the need for a whole new Constitution to be introduced:

'In the year which sees the 50th anniversary of our Constitution, the most appropriate manner in which to mark this milestone would be an all-party agreement to draft a new Constitution that would perpetuate the best of the 1937 version but make provision for Ireland, the men, the women and the families of the eighties and into the future.'

Deputy Lenihan replied:

'The reason we have chosen the basic amendment for the House is because of the point the Senator [Robinson] has raised . . . The main matter requires to be dealt with in a further constitutional amendment embodying the aspect of where the Executive authority lies in the conduct of foreign affairs, in the area of past treaties and future agreements.'

The Second Stage passed by 47 votes to 6. In the Committee and Final Stages, amendments were put and lost on division. The Bill passed without division.

The referendum took place on 26 May 1987. As prescribed by the Referendum (Amendment) Act, 1987, the polling card stated:

THE TENTH AMENDMENT OF THE CONSTITUTION BILL, 1987, proposes to enable the State to ratify the Single European Act by inserting the sentence here following into subsection 3° of section 3 of Article 29 of the Constitution after the first sentence: [text as per Act quoted]

Total electorate		2,461,790
Total poll		1,085,304
Percentage poll		44.1%
Votes in favour	755,423	[69.92%]
Votes against	324,977	[30.08%]
Spoiled votes		4,904

The Bill was carried in all constituencies.
The Bill was signed by the President on 22 June 1987.

TENTH AMENDMENT OF THE CONSTITUTION ACT, 1987

AN ACT TO AMEND THE CONSTITUTION
[*22 June 1987*]

WHEREAS by virtue of Article 46 of the Constitution any provision of the Constitution may be amended in the manner provided by that Article:

AND WHEREAS it is proposed to amend Article 29 of the Constitution:

BE IT THEREFORE ENACTED BY THE OIREACHTAS AS FOLLOWS:

1. Article 29 of the Constitution is hereby amended as follows:
   (*a*) the sentence set out in *Part I* of the Schedule to this Act shall be inserted in subsection 3° of section 4 of the Irish text after the first sentence.
   (*b*) the sentence set out in *Part II* of the Schedule to this Act shall be inserted in subsection 3° of section 4 of the English text after the first sentence.

2. (1) The amendment of the Constitution effected by this Act shall be called the Tenth Amendment of the Constitution.

   (2) This Act may be cited as the Tenth Amendment of the Constitution Act, 1987.

SCHEDULE
Part II

The State may ratify the Single European Act (signed on behalf of the Member States of the Communities at Luxembourg on the 17th day of February, 1986, and at The Hague on the 28th day of February, 1986).

ELEVENTH AMENDMENT ACT — OIREACHTAS DEBATES

DÁIL ÉIREANN

The Second Stage of the Eleventh Amendment of the Constitution Bill, 1992, began in Dáil Éireann on 5 May 1992. The only political party to oppose the Bill was Democratic Left. Although the Bill is enabling only, the vast bulk of the debate especially in the Second Stage was about the substantive issue of the ratification of the Maastricht Treaty and the merits of the Treaty itself. The Second Stage debate dealt with unemployment and other matters. The most troubled part of the debate related to Protocol 17 of the Treaty of European Union under which Article 40.3.3 of the Constitution [as created by the Eight Amendment of the Constitution] was protected from being affected by the Treaty, and a subsequent Solemn Declaration by the High Contracting Parties to the Treaty that, following the entry into force of the Treaty, they would be favourably disposed to amending the Protocol to extend its application to a future constitutional amendment of that Article if Ireland so requests. The Committee Stage was very brief.

The Bill was introduced by the Taoiseach, Albert Reynolds:

'The text of this Bill to amend our Constitution is simple, straightforward and limited solely to enabling the State to ratify the treaty on European Union signed at Maastricht on 7 February last and become a member of this Union, as well as enabling the State to ratify the Agreement relating to Community Patents of 15 December 1989, between the member states of the Communities. The form of the amendment is the same as in 1987, except that there is a reference to European Union as well as to the Communities, and to bodies competent under the Community Treaties, such as the

European Monetary Institute to be established at Stage 2 of European Monetary Union. They do not include Western European Union . . . The Community Patents Agreement was signed by Ireland in 1989. Because the Agreement was concluded inter-governmentally and is thus not necessitated by the obligations of EC membership, provisions which conflict with the supremacy of Irish courts would not be covered under our Constitution . . . Ratification will be completed by all our partners before the end of this year, in some cases well ahead of target . . . No insurmountable problems are foreseen in the other member states.'

The Taoiseach then went on to canvas the economic benefits of the Treaty. He also argued that just as the EEC went ahead with the Social Charter and with the EMS without all its members, so it could go ahead with Maastricht without Ireland. He also outlined the merits of the Treaty for the rights of workers, women's rights, the cohesion fund and the environment, while setting out his view that neutrality was not an issue in the Treaty. He concluded:

'When we were in Opposition in 1986, we argued for a referendum on the Single European Act. There has been no argument about having a referendum now, and similarly in the future, if further fundamental changes in the Community or in the Union need to be approved. Regular consultation of the people is the foundation of the strong pro-European consensus that we have.'

He was opposed by Deputy J. O'Keeffe who moved an amendment:

'To delete "now" and to add "at the end of the motion this day two weeks provided that in the meantime the Government has initiated a Government Bill or the Dáil has approved at Second Stage a Private Members' Bill, to amend the Constitution providing that Article 40.3.3° of the Constitution shall not be invoked to prohibit or interfere with the exercise of the right to travel to or from the State for the purpose of receiving services lawfully available in other jurisdictions or to obtain, within the State, counselling and information relating to such services subject to such restriction as may be provided by law".'

The particular 'service' in question was abortion, a matter which played a large part in the Oireachtas and public debates on the Amendment. Deputy O'Keeffe, however, was able to confirm the positive response of Fine Gael to the Taoiseach's request for support for the Community Patents Agreement. Despite his opposing motion Deputy O'Keeffe went on to say:

'As a people we should be proud to be Irish in Europe. We should vote yes to the Treaty on European Union because, taking a calm and balanced view, it is in the best interests of our people to do so . . . My criticism of the Fianna Fáil–Progressive Democrats Government and the tabling by me of an amendment to the Bill is not because we in Fine Gael are opposed to the Bill. On the contrary, this approach was adopted because we are so committed to European Union. In particular, we are concerned that the referendum on 18 June to ratify the change in the Constitution may be put at risk because of confusion on the travel and information issues.'

Deputy Spring for the Labour Party supported the Bill:

'In the detailed analysis of Maastricht prepared by the Labour Party which is being published today the party recommended that the people of Ireland should vote

yes to Maastricht. However we are going further than
that. We are calling for a substantial campaign by the
Irish Government backed up by the whole community
to make the Treaty work for every citizen of Europe . . .
for many citizens, this whole debate will be
overshadowed by the issues of travel and information
brought up by the outcome of the "X" case . . . Protocol
17 was inserted at the request of the Irish Government
precisely to protect the operation of Article 40.3.3°, and
the result is this: in normal circumstances, EC law
would almost certainly over-rule any attempt to prevent
a woman from travelling abroad for purposes lawful in
the Community. The effect of the Protocol is certainly
to prevent any European Court challenge to the law on
abortion in Ireland.'

(In the 'X' case the Supreme Court held that a woman had a
right to an abortion if her pregnancy posed a real and
substantial threat to her life, including a threat from suicide.)
Deputy Spring also said:

'I do not believe that acceptance of the Maastricht
Treaty poses imminent dangers to our neutrality,
notwith-standing reservations about the as yet
unresolved future roles of both Western European
Union and NATO.'

Wider issues were raised by Deputy M. Higgins:

'Will there be legislation or a constitutional referendum
[on monetary and economic proposals]? Equally in
relation to this extraordinary Bill before us, Part II,
Paragraph 5° states: "No provision of this Constitution
invalidates laws enacted . . . acts done or measures
adopted by the European Union or by the Communities
or by institutions thereof". That also applied to the
Single European Act, but this Bill adds: "or by bodies

competent under the Treaties establishing the Communities, from having the force of law in the State". What bodies are they? Is it the European Central Bank or the Western European Union?'

When the Second Stage resumed on 6 May 1992 Deputy Lenihan, for the Government, argued:

'Sovereignty is an idle, sterile concept in itself. What is important is the exercise of sovereignty in the national interest. Our people exercised their sovereignty in ratifying the decision of the Oireachtas to go into Europe on 1 January 1973. The European Union Treaty is a further stage along that road.'

The Minister of State at the Department of the Taoiseach, Deputy T. Kitt explained the difficulties attendant on attempting to amend the Treaty:

'Part . . . of the amendment put forward by Deputy De Rossa and others proposes that the Maastricht Treaty should be renegotiated . . . It is not an option. The EC General Affairs Council held in Luxembourg on 6 April has already made it clear that they will not reopen the Maastricht Treaty or its Protocols because to do so could leave the way open to pressures in other member states for other amendments.'

On 7 May 1992 the Second Stage resumed and Deputy Andrews stated:

'I regret that Deputy De Rossa and others appear to attach no value to the Solemn Declaration. I do not know how he can reject a document which has been accepted by all of the signatories to the Treaty . . . Deputy Michael D. Higgins and others raised the question of the competent bodies under the Treaties establishing the Communities in subsection 5 of the draft amendment. The competent bodies are the European Central Bank and the European Monetary Institute which is to be established at the beginning of the second stage of European Monetary Union . . . I wish to make it clear that a common defence policy would require another negotiation; and there is provision in the Treaty for another intergovernmental conference in 1996 to negotiate any amendments to the Treaties that might be necessary. Any such amendments would, as the Taoiseach pointed out on Wednesday, require to be ratified here by referendum of the Irish people. This will remain the situation after ratification of the Treaty on European Union.'

The Second Stage passed by 69 votes to 66, and the Committee and Final Stages were taken the same day. Deputy De Rossa proposed amendments which would have separated the three parts of the Bill into three separate amendments. Deputy Andrews replied:

'The Government could not agree to separate subsections 4° and 5° as both are necessary to enable Ireland to ratify the Treaty and take on the obligations of membership.'

He then gave a brief defence of the patents clause. Deputy Garland moved an amendment:

'To delete "of the European Union or" . . . I have entered this fundamental change to the proposed amendment to the Constitution on the basis of advice I have been receiving concerning its unnecessarily wide scope . . . Anything that may reasonably be interpreted to fall within the very vague objectives of the Union will be immune now to legal challenge and therefore will not need a further referendum. This makes nonsense out of the Government claim that we will have to have a referendum on defence aspects of 1996.

Furthermore, the Union will be able to evolve new labour laws, emigration rules, extradition treaties, cross-Border hot pursuit, European identification systems and so on without reference to the Irish people ... The areas of the Union which are intergovernmental and not subject to the European Court of Justice, mainly security and justice, are being removed from the ambit of the Irish courts as well by virtue of this amendment.'

Deputy Andrews replied:

'The subsection permits the laws, acts and measures adopted by the European Union, by the Communities or by bodies competent under the Communities such as the new Central Bank, to have the force of law in Ireland as this is required by our Treaty obligations.'

The Bill passed all stages in the Dáil without amendment.

SEANAD ÉIREANN

The Eleventh Amendment of the Constitution Bill, 1992, Second Stage was introduced in Seanad Éireann on 14 May 1992. There was, in general, all-party agreement on the basic merits of the proposal, but abortion, the problem with Protocol 17 and the subsequent Solemn Declaration by the High Contracting Parties to the Treaty, created considerable controversy. Other issues which were raised included the standards of the roads, the Culliton Report on industrial reorganisation, and defence policy. On introducing the Bill, the Taoiseach said:

'The text of this Bill to amend our Constitution is simple, straightforward and limited solely to enabling the State to ratify the Treaty of European Union signed at Maastricht on 7 February last and become a member of this Union, as well as enabling the State to ratify the Agreement relating to Community Patents of 15 December 1989, between the Member States of the Communities.'

The Taoiseach then set out the merits of the Treaties along the lines of his Dáil speech. The major speech in opposition to the Bill came from a member of the Government, Senator Hanafin:

'I am going to oppose this Bill and in doing so I differ with my party and my colleagues. I regret differing with my colleagues and it is, therefore, necessary for me to explain as simply as I can my reasons for taking this course. These reasons have to do with the clear implications of the Maastricht Treaty for abortion law in Ireland, and for our ability in the future to vote effectively to protect the rights of life before birth . . . We are also being asked to approve Article 29.4.5⁰ [in the amending text] which has consequences going far beyond the mere ratification of Maastricht . . . Were we not certain, whatever our views, that as a result of the referendum, abortion could not be legalised in Ireland without a further decision by the people? I do not think it unreasonable to say that this was a perverse decision . . . I do not believe we got it wrong in 1983, but the amendment we then enacted to prevent abortion has been misread to allow it. To say that we cannot correct it would be to say we cannot find the words with which to rule out the intentional killing of unborn children without, at the same time, interfering with the medical practice of over a century. This is nonsense; of course, it can be done.'

Another side of the debate was taken by Professor Murphy:

'the new Treaty proposes to give powers to the European Union far beyond what is necessary to endorse the Treaty and that there are Titles in the Union which will not be amenable not alone to our courts but to the European courts.'

When the Second Stage was resumed on 15 May 1992, the point was taken up by Senator Norris:

'But the Government's proposal to give, in addition, the force of constitutional obligation to whatever is necessitated by membership of the European Union means that matters arising under Treaty Title V, which deals with common, foreign and security policy, and Title VI which deals with co-operation, in justice and home affairs, are now quite unexpectedly, being made immune to constitutional challenge in Irish law even though they are not, or not yet, within the compass of European law . . . In the case of extra-Community acts of the union, there is no Community or no Union court authorised to exercise such jurisdiction. The result is that no court would be empowered to hear a complaint about the effects of such law or acts of the union in Ireland.'

The Second Stage passed by 41 votes to 4. The Committee and Final Stages were taken on the same day. In the debate on the Committee Stage Senator B. Ryan pointed out that:

'The problem is that anything that is agreed unanimously [at intergovernmental conference] under Titles V and VI of the Treaty of European Union is neither subject to review within the European Court of Justice nor, because of the ham-fisted wording of this amendment, subject to review by the Irish Supreme Court.'

Senator Daly made a similar point:

'In fact, it is clear from the judgment that future Treaty amendments involving significant concessions of sovereignty or containing threats to fundamental constitutional rights were regarded by the Supreme Court in the Crotty case as not within the licence to agree to the future Treaty amendments contained in the 1972 amendment. It must be remembered, however, that the interpretation of the amendments proposed in the forthcoming referendum would be a matter for the Irish courts, not for the Irish Government. Any Irish Government, which assumed that, on the basis of the present amendment, they could undertake a defence policy or a common defence which undermined the sovereignty of the State in these areas without a further referendum would be rash indeed.'

The question was carried and all stages were passed.

The referendum took place on 18 June 1992. As prescribed by the Referendum (Amendment) Act, 1992, the polling card stated:

THE ELEVENTH AMENDMENT OF THE CONSTITUTION BILL, 1992, relating to the amendment of Article 29 of the Constitution proposes to repeal the third sentence in subsection 3° of section 4 thereof and to insert the subsections here following into the said section 4: [There followed the sub-sections numbered 4°, 5° and 6° in the Bill.]

Total electorate		2,542,840
Total poll		1,457,219
Percentage poll		57.3%
Votes in favour	1,001,076	[69.06%]
Votes against	448,655	[30.94%]
Spoiled votes		7,488

The Bill was carried in all constituencies.

The Bill was signed by the President on 16 July 1992.

ELEVENTH AMENDMENT OF THE CONSTITUTION ACT, 1992

AN ACT TO AMEND THE CONSTITUTION
[*16 July 1992*]

WHEREAS by virtue of Article 46 of the Constitution any provision of the Constitution may be amended in the manner provided by that Article:

AND WHEREAS it is proposed to amend Article 29 of the Constitution:

BE IT THEREFORE ENACTED BY THE OIREACHTAS AS FOLLOWS:

1. Article 29.4 of the Constitution is hereby amended as follows:
    (*a*) by the repeal of the third sentence in subsection 3° of section 4 of the Irish text and by the insertion of the text set out in *Part I* of the Schedule to this Act;
    (*b*) by the the[100] repeal of the third sentence in subsection 3° of section 4 of the English text and by the insertion of the text set out in *Part II* of the Schedule to this Act.

2. (1) The amendment of the Constitution effected by this Act shall be called the Eleventh Amendment of the Constitution.

    (2) This Act may be cited as the Eleventh Amendment of the Constitution Act, 1992.

---

100. Thus.

SCHEDULE
Part II

4° The State may ratify the Treaty on European Union signed at Maastricht on the 7th day of February, 1992, and may become a member of that Union.

5° No provision of this Constitution invalidates laws enacted, acts done or measures adopted by the State which are necessitated by the obligations of membership of the European Union or of the Communities, or prevents laws enacted, acts done or measures adopted by the European Union or by the Communities or by institutions thereof, or by bodies competent under the Treaties establishing the Communities, from having the force of law in the State.

6° The State may ratify the Agreement relating to Community Patents drawn up between the Member States of the Communities and done at Luxembourg on the 15th day of December, 1989.

TWELFTH, THIRTEENTH & FOURTEENTH AMENDMENTS OF THE CONSTITUTION BILLS — OIREACHTAS DEBATES

DÁIL ÉIREANN

The Twelfth Amendment of the Constitution Bill, 1992, was introduced in Dáil Éireann by the Government under Taoiseach Albert Reynolds. The Second Stage began in the Dáil on 20 October 1992. Although primarily related to the Twelfth Amendment Bill, under the Order of Business the debate was explicitly about the Thirteenth Amendment Bill and the Fourteenth Amendment Bill also. The debate was, in many respects, a re-run of the 1983 debate but at a much lower intensity and with much greater courtesy. It centred largely on the merits of the Twelfth Amendment Bill in relation to abortion. In particular the question was raised if the distinction between health and life could or would pose a threat to the life of pregnant women. The only issue raised concerning the Constitution as such was whether such a matter should or should not be treated in the Constitution at all, and that issue was not really discussed in depth in the Second Stage. In the Committee Stage the question of consequential legislation was resurrected.

The Second Stage was resumed on 21 October and, unusually, ran into the early hours of 22 October 1992. The debate resumed on the morning of the 22 October and the Second Stage passed without amendment.

On 27 October 1992 the Committee and Final Stages were taken and all stages passed by 68 votes to 57.

SEANAD ÉIREANN

The debate began in the Seanad on 28 October 1992. As agreed on the Order of Business, the three Amendment Bills were taken together for the purpose of debate, following the procedure used in the Dáil. This had the odd consequence that the Thirteenth and Fourteenth Amendment Bills were debated before being introduced. The Minister for Justice, Deputy Flynn, introducing the debate said:

> 'Each of the three Bills proposes to amend subsection (3) of section 3 of Article 40 of the Constitution and their combined effect would be to deal with the various issues that arise from the decision of the Supreme Court in *(The) Attorney General v X*[101] and some other Supreme Court decisions on Article 40.3.3⁰ in so far as it relates to provision of information . . . The importance the Government attach to the need to protect the life of the mother is the reason we have not been able to accept the amendment put forward by the Pro-life Campaign . . . Pro-life groups make much of the distinction between direct and indirect termination mainly on the basis that an indirect termination is an unintended effect of other treatment . . . As a matter of law foreseen consequences of an act are, of course, intended.'

The Bills were opposed by a member of the Government side of the Seanad, Senator Hanafin, who said:

> 'How much of a risk is a real and substantial one? All risks are real, no matter how small; but the assessment of what constitutes a substantial risk will always be highly subjective. A substantial risk may be well short of a major risk. If the Minister for Justice were told, God forbid, that there was a 5 per cent chance that he would be involved in an accident on the way home to Castlebar this weekend, I think he would rightly regard that as a very substantial risk indeed. What about a 1 per cent risk?'

---

101. *(The) Attorney General v 'X' and Others* 1992 IR(2) 1; 1992 ILRM 401.

The debate resumed on 29 October 1992. Senator Norris made the claim:

> 'We have a Constitution, the Constitution of 1937, of which we can be proud.'

The Second Stage passed without amendment.
The Committee and Final Stages were taken on 30 October 1992 and all stages passed.

Thirteenth Amendment Act

DÁIL ÉIREANN

In the meantime, in Dáil Éireann on 22 October 1992, between midnight and one o'clock in the morning, the Thirteenth Amendment of the Constitution Bill, 1992, Second Stage was introduced by the Minister for Justice, Deputy Flynn.

The question was put immediately and agreed to without discussion. Later in the morning, shortly after 10.30 a.m., the Committee and Final Stages were taken. In the debate the major point made was that the Bill was not necessary as the right to travel already existed in the unamended Constitution. All stages passed.

SEANAD ÉIREANN

On 29 October 1992 the Thirteenth Amendment of the Constitution Bill, 1992, Second Stage was introduced and immediately passed, having been debated together with the Twelfth Amendment Bill. The Committee and Final Stages were taken on 30 October 1992. In the debate Senator Costello moved an amendment to include movement within the State which was opposed by the Minister of State at the Department of Justice, Deputy O'Dea, on the grounds that:

> 'the suggested amendment seems to assume that there is no general right to travel under the Constitution. I am unable to agree that there is no existing constitutional right to travel.'

All stages of the Bill passed.

Fourteenth Amendment Act

DÁIL ÉIREANN

In the Dáil on 22 October 1992, in the early hours of the morning, the Fourteenth Amendment of the Constitution Bill, 1992, Second Stage, was taken. There was some debate on the distinction between information and counselling, between directive or non-directive, and what the Minister intended to put into his proposed consequential legislation. The Committee Stage was also taken at that time. All stages passed.

SEANAD ÉIREANN

On 29 October 1992, the Fourteenth Amendment of the Constitution Bill, 1992, Second Stage was introduced and immediately passed, having been debated together with the Twelfth Amendment Bill. The subsequent stages were taken on 30 October 1992 and all were passed.

The referendum took place on 25 November 1992. As prescribed by the Referendum (Amendment) (No.2) Act, 1992, the polling card stated:

You may vote at the Referenda on three proposals

White Ballot Paper—Right to Life

THE TWELFTH AMENDMENT OF THE CONSTITUTION BILL, 1992, proposes to amend Article 40 of the Constitution by the addition of the text here following to subsection 3^0 of section 3 thereof:

'It shall be unlawful to terminate the life of an unborn unless such termination is necessary to save the life, as distinct from the health, of the mother where there is an illness or disorder of the mother giving rise to a real and substantial risk to her life, not being a risk of self-destruction.'

Green Ballot Paper—Travel

THE THIRTEENTH AMENDMENT OF THE CONSTITUTION BILL, 1992, proposes to amend Article 40 of the Constitution by the addition of the paragraph here following to subsection 3^0 of section 3 thereof:

'This subsection shall not limit freedom to travel between the State and another state.'

Pink Ballot Paper—Information

THE FOURTEENTH AMENDMENT OF THE CONSTITUTION BILL, 1992, proposes to amend Article 40 of the Constitution by the addition of the paragraph here following to subsection 3^0 of section 3 thereof:

'This subsection shall not limit freedom to obtain or make available in the State, subject to such conditions as may be laid down by law, information relating to services lawfully available in another state.'

Twelfth Amendment of the Constitution Bill, 1992.

Total electorate		2,542,841
Total poll		1,733,309
Percentage poll		68.2%
Votes in favour	572,177	[34.6%]
Votes against	1,079,297	[65.4%]
Spoiled votes		81,835

Thirteenth Amendment of the Constitution Bill, 1992.

Total electorate		2,542,841
Total poll		1,733,821
Percentage poll		68.2%
Votes in favour	1,035,308	[62.4%]
Votes against	624,059	[37.6%]
Spoiled votes		74,454

Fourteenth Amendment of the Constitution Bill, 1992.

Total electorate		2,542,841
Total poll		1,732,433
Percentage poll		68.1%
Votes in favour	992,833	[59.9%]
Votes against	665,106	[40.1%]
Spoiled votes		74,494

The Twelfth Amendment of the Constitution Bill, 1992, was not approved by the people.

The Thirteenth Amendment of the Constitution Bill, 1992, and the Fourteenth Amendment of the Constitution Bill, 1992, were approved by the people and both Bills were signed by the President on 23 December 1992.

THIRTEENTH AMENDMENT OF THE CONSTITUTION ACT, 1992

AN ACT TO AMEND THE CONSTITUTION.
[*23 December 1992*]

WHEREAS by virtue of Article 46 of the Constitution any provision of the Constitution may be amended in the manner provided by that Article:

AND WHEREAS it is proposed to amend Article 40.3 of the Constitution:

BE IT THEREFORE ENACTED BY THE OIREACHTAS AS FOLLOWS:

1. Article 40.3 of the Constitution is hereby amended as follows:
   (*a*) in subsection 3° of the Irish text, of a second paragraph the text of which is set out in *Part I* of the Schedule to this Act;
   (*b*) in subsection 3° of the English text, of a second paragraph the text of which is set out in *Part II* of the Schedule to this Act.

2. (1) The amendment of the Constitution effected by this Act shall be called the Thirteenth Amendment of the Constitution.

   (2) This Act may be cited as the Thirteenth Amendment of the Constitution Act, 1992.

SCHEDULE
Part II

This subsection shall not limit freedom to travel between the State and another state.

FOURTEENTH AMENDMENT OF THE CONSTITUTION ACT, 1992

AN ACT TO AMEND THE CONSTITUTION
[*23 December 1992*]

WHEREAS by virtue of Article 46 of the Constitution any provision of the Constitution may be amended in the manner provided by that Article:

AND WHEREAS it is proposed to amend Article 40.3 of the Constitution:

BE IT THEREFORE ENACTED BY THE OIREACHTAS AS FOLLOWS:

1. Article 40.3 of the Constitution is hereby amended by the addition thereto, immediately before section 4—
   (*a*) in subsection 3° of the Irish text, of a paragraph the text of which is set out in *Part I* of the Schedule to this Act;
   (*b*) in subsection 3° of the English text, of a paragraph the text of which is set out in *Part II* of the Schedule to this Act.

2. (1) The amendment of the Constitution effected by this Act shall be called the Fourteenth Amendment of the Constitution.

   (2) This Act may be cited as the Fourteenth Amendment of the Constitution Act, 1992.

SCHEDULE
Part II

This subsection shall not limit freedom to obtain or make available, in the State, subject to such conditions as may be laid down by law, information relating to services lawfully available in another state.

Appendices

APPENDIX 1

DEVELOPMENT OF JUDICIAL AWARENESS OF THE CONSTITUTION OF IRELAND (BUNREACHT NA hÉIREANN) AS THE *GRUNDNORM* OF THE IRISH LEGAL SYSTEM

Any indepth commentary, much less analysis, of the development of judicial thinking in regard to the evident increasing cognisance on the part of the Irish judiciary of the nature of the Constitution as the *Grundnorm*[102] of our legal system, or indeed of the strides made in this area over the years, is beyond the scope of this work. It is also true to say that the Constitution as *Grundnorm*, Kelsen's concept of that primary source of law from which all other law in any particular polity derives authority, has not yet been established in the popular consciousness.

The Irish judiciary initially tended to display a large degree of caution in using the Bunreacht at least until such time as the new Constitution was placed beyond the power of the Oireachtas to amend it (i.e. once the three-year period during which it was capable of amendment by that institution had passed).

The extent of this general wariness in the judicial attitude may be traced back to the effects of the insertion of Article 2(a) in the Constitution of 1922, inserted by virtue of the Constitution (Amendment No. 17) Act, 1931.[103] The effects of this Amendment have already been discussed in the Introduction.[104]

---

102. In this context *Grundnorm* refers to the primary source of the validity of laws of any polity, that is, the source beyond which we need not delve to discover the fountainhead of law in the polity; that from which all valid law essentially derives.
103. No. 37 of 1931.
104. Introduction p.9.

Modern judicial opinion recognises that there are certain fundamental precepts of natural law which may not be violated or negated by the legislative process. In 1935 in *(The) State (Ryan) v Lennon*[105], Kennedy C.J. in his notable dissenting judgment, had this to say:

'The net effect, then, is that the Oireachtas has taken judicial power from the Judiciary and handed it to the Executive, and has surrendered its own trust as a legislature to the Executive Council, in respect of the extensive area of matters covered by the Appendix to the Article. Remembering that the "Tribunal" is to consist of five persons holding commissions as commandants (or higher ranks) issued to them by, and held at the pleasure of the Executive Council, and holding membership of the "Tribunal" at the will of the Executive Council, the result of the Article clearly is that whenever any Executive Council thinks it expedient to use the Article, that Council itself prosecutes (in pursuance of its proper function) a person charged by it with an offence (which may be an offence brought within the scope of the Article by an Executive Minister's signature) and conducts the prosecution itself, "trying" the charge by its own removable nominees, and itself convicts the accused person, by the same convenient and decorous machinery, and prescribes any sentence for the individual case it chooses through the same convenient and decorous machinery. Every act, from the arrest of the individual and the charging him with an "offence" to the sentence and its execution, is, therefore, in naked reality, the act of the Executive Council.'

Kennedy C.J., referring to the powers contained in Article 2(a) in the context of replying to a submission by counsel for the defendant which proposed that there were certain fundamental laws (i.e. retroactive penal sanctions in this

105. 1935 IR 170; 69 ILTR 125.

instance) the promulgation of which were not within the ambit of the Oireachtas, had this to say about the provision:

> '[The provision was] in substance and practical effect repugnant to the principle and the almost universal practice which forbids retroactive penal legalisation. It is within the application of the words of Alexander Hamilton, writing in *The Federalist*, No. LXXXIV: "The creation of crimes after the commission of the fact or, in other words, the subjecting of men to punishment for things which, when done, were breaches of no law, and the practice of arbitrary imprisonments, have been, in all ages, the favourite and most formal instruments of tyranny."'

In the same case, Murnaghan J., while feeling himself bound to dismiss the appeal in question, nonetheless referred to 'the extreme rigour' of Article 2(a) and said that the provisions of the Article:

> 'pass far beyond anything having the semblance of legal procedure, and the judicial mind is staggered at the very complete departure from legal methods used in these courts.'

Fitzgibbon J., in this case, was also quite clear as to his view of the state of the law prior to the insertion of Article 2(a) when he said:

> 'By the common law which existed for centuries before the Free State was constituted, statements or confessions obtained from an accused party by threats or inducements held out by persons in authority could not be given in evidence against him, and the maxim *Nemo tenetur se ipsum accusare* [no one is bound to

incriminate himself] was rigidly enforced by the judges. When the Constitution of the Free State was framed that law was continued in force here by Article 73.'

Nonetheless the Court, by a two to one majority, held that the amendment to the Constitution and the consequent setting up of Military Tribunals was within the power of the Oireachtas. At this stage, the judiciary had reached a point where they were patently admitting their powerlessness in the face of the ability and indeed the obvious willingness of the Oireachtas to render the Constitution of 1922 largely meaningless. It must be borne in mind that during all of the time it was in operation—some fifteen years—the Constitution remained capable of amendment by ordinary legislation.[106] If the judiciary had reached a point by the mid-thirties where they considered that they had, to a large extent, been rendered powerless in many respects to counter even the most draconian amendments of the 1922 Constitution and the legislation which was consequent on these amendments, it is not surprising that initially they took a distant view of the Bunreacht, at least during the first years of its existence. This attitude demonstrates quite clearly that certain laws passed by the Oireachtas had come to be viewed as the *Grundnorm*, for the Oireachtas had acquired the power to pass legislation which would otherwise not have been acceptable.

During the 1940s and early 1950s, very little Constitutional case law was produced by the Courts, with the notable exceptions of *Buckley v The Attorney General*[107] and *(In re) Tilson, Infants*[108] (Gavan Duffy P. and affirmed in the Supreme Court by a majority—this case concerned the respective rights of parents in regard to the religious education of their children).

Gavan Duffy J. was the only judge who was willing to have recourse to the provisions of the Constitution. For example, as early as 1950, in *Buckley v The Attorney General* ('the

---

106. See Introduction.
107. 1950 IR 67.
108. 1951 IR 1; 86 ILTR 49; see also the earlier case of *(In re) Frost, Infants*, 1947 IR 3; 82 ILTR 24 and also *(In re) Keenan, Infants*, 84 ILTR 169.

Sinn Féin Funds Case')[109], he analysed the whole area of the separation of powers and judicial independence. In that case, while conceding that the Sinn Féin Funds Act, 1947 had probably been passed for the best of motives, he went on to say:

> '[but] I cannot lose sight of the constitutional separation of powers. This Court cannot, in deference to an Act of the Oireachtas, abdicate its proper jurisdiction to administer justice and therefore it cannot dismiss the pending action without hearing the plaintiffs.'

And he continued:

> 'this action is not stayed unless and until it is stayed by a judicial order of the High Court of Justice; the payment out of the funds in Court requires a judicial order of this Court, and under the Constitution no other organ of State is competent to determine how the High Court of Justice shall dispose of the issues raised by the pleadings in this action.'

On appeal by the Attorney General to the Supreme Court, O'Byrne J. delivering the judgment of the Court, described the action of the Oireachtas as an attempt by the Oireachtas to determine the dispute, and said:

> 'In our opinion this is clearly repugnant to the provisions of the Constitution, as being an unwarrantable interference by the Oireachtas with the operations of the courts in a purely judicial domain.[110]'

---

109. 1950 IR 67; see also *Buckley v The Attorney General* (No. 2), 84 ILTR 9.
110. It is also interesting to note how Ó Dalaigh C.J. in the later case of *Melling v O'Mathghamha* viewed this whole matter when he said:
> 'If our Constitution and the Constitution of Saorstat Éireann both have adopted the theory of the tripartite separation of the powers of government with express limitations on the powes alike of Legislature and Executive over the citizen, the reason is not unconnected with our previous experience under an alien government whose parliament was omnipotent and in whose executive lay wide reserves of prerogative power.'

In the earlier case of *Pigs Marketing Board v Donnelly*[111], Hanna J. stated quite clearly that an Act of the Oireachtas would be presumed to be Constitutional unless repugnancy could be clearly established. The reasoning underlying this principle was restated in Buckley's case by O'Byrne J. in delivering the judgment of the Supreme Court:

> 'In our opinion [this] springs from, and is necessitated by, that respect which one great organ of the State owes to another.'

One case which appears to have taken a somewhat backward step is that of *The Attorney General v Southern Industrial Trust*[112] where Lavery J. cautioned against putting forward submissions based on findings of the Court on previous occasions where the constitutionality of an Act was sought to be impugned, when he said:

> 'where this Court has examined the provisions of any particular Act or Bill and pronounced on its validity or invalidity, it is not always helpful to rely on the decision in another case because particular provisions of the law there in question may have determined the decision.
>   Statements of principle are, of course, decisive and binding, but otherwise such decisions do not help and particularly decisions on laws impugned as violating different Articles of the Constitution.'

Here the Court went to great lengths to distinguish its decision in this case from its decision in *Buckley v The Attorney General*[113]—in the context of Article 43 of the Constitution. This case led to some degree of uncertainty and indeed the decision was followed to some degree by

---

111. 1939 IR 413. This was the first case in which a statute was challenged under the Bunreacht.
112. 94 ILTR 161.
113. 1950 IR 67.

O'Keeffe J. in *East Donegal Cooperative v The Attorney General*[114]. The matter appears to have been finally laid to rest by Kenny J. in *Central Dublin Development Association v The Attorney General*[115]. All of these cases concerned the rights accruing to private property and are merely cited to demonstrate to some degree the fact that *Southern Industrial Trust* was to be viewed with some doubt. The verdict in this case was also found unacceptable in *Blake v The Attorney General*[116] to the extent that the property rights contained in Article 40.3 were the same as those contained in Article 43.

The great modern development of our constitutional law over the past thirty years or so commenced in 1965 with *Ryan v The Attorney General* ('The Fluoridation Case')[117]. This case would appear to have been the great turning point which has led to the acceptance of the Constitution as the *Grundnorm* of our legal system. This case established the existence of the so called 'unenumerated' personal rights contained in Article 40.3 of the Constitution.

Since that decision, the Courts have come to recognise a whole range of rights which they have declared to exist under this Article.

In that case, Kenny J., while holding against the plaintiff in the particular context of her claim, stated that if Article 40.3 (i.e. the general guarantee contained therein) extended to cover personal rights other than those specified, then:

'the High Court and the Supreme Court have the difficult and responsible duty of ascertaining and declaring what are the personal rights of the citizen

---

114. 1970 IR 317; 104 ILTR 81.
115. 109 ILTR 69.
116. 1982 IR 117.
117. 1965 IR 294.

which are guaranteed by the Constitution. In modern times this would seem to be a function of the legislative rather than the judicial; but it was done by the courts in the formative period of the common law and there is no reason why they should not do it now.

A number of factors indicate that the guarantee is not confined to the rights specified in Article 40 but extends to other personal rights of the citizen. Firstly, there is sub-section 2 of section 3 of Article 40 . . . The words "in particular" show that sub-section 2 is a detailed statement of something which is already contained in sub-section 1 of the general guarantee. But sub-section 2 refers to rights in connection with life and good name and there are no rights connected with those two matters specified in Article 40. It follows, I think, that the general guarantee in sub-section 1 must extend to rights not specified in Article 40.

Secondly, there are many personal rights of the citizen which follow from the Christian and democratic nature of the State which are not mentioned in Article 40 at all—the right to free movement within the State and the right to marry are examples of this. This also leads to the conclusion that the general guarantee extends to rights not specified in Article 40.

In my opinion, one of the personal rights of the citizen protected by the general guarantee is the right to bodily integrity. I understand the right to bodily integrity to mean that no mutilation of the body or any of its members may be carried out on any citizen under the authority of the law except for the good of the whole body and that no process which is or may, as a matter of probability, be dangerous or harmful to the life or health of the citizens or any of them may be imposed (in the sense of being made compulsory) by an Act of the Oireachtas.'

Upholding the views of Kenny J. the Supreme Court stated:

'The Court agrees with Mr Justice Kenny that the "personal rights" mentioned in section 3.1 are not exhausted by the enumeration of "life, person, good name, and property rights" in section 3.2 as shown by the words "in particular"; nor by the more detached treatment of specific rights in the subsequent sections of the Article. To attempt to make a list of all the rights which may properly fall within the category of "personal rights" would be difficult and, fortunately, is unnecessary in this present case.'

The Court, therefore, ensured that the category of personal rights was by no means closed and since that time there have been numerous cases in which the courts have added to this list of rights. These are far too numerous to be considered here, save to say that they have included such rights as the right not to have one's health put at risk by the State—*The State (Richardson) v The Governor of Mountjoy Prison*[119]; the right to marital privacy—*McGee v The Attorney General*[120]; the right to earn a livelihood—*Murtagh Properties v Cleary*[121]; the right to fair procedures—*The State (Healy) v Donoghue*[122]; the right to litigate—*Macauly v The Minister for Posts and Telegraphs*[123] and *Byrne v Ireland*[124]; the right to travel—*The*

---

119. Unrep.: High Court (Barrington J.) 28/3/1980.
120. 1974 IR 284; 109 ILTR 29. See also *Norris v Attorney General;* 1984 IR 36.
121. 1972 IR 330.
122. 1976 IR 325; 110 ILTR 9.
123. 1966 IR 345.
124. 1972 IR 241.

State (M) v The Attorney General[125]; personal right of an unmarried mother in regard to her child—*G. v An Bord Uchtála*[126].

The foregoing constitute only a short list of the better known cases in this area and they demonstrate the willingness of the Courts to engage in the development of just one particular area. It is stressed that the list is far from complete.

A point to note concerns the 1954 case of *The State (Killian) v The Minister for Justice*[127] in which the then Supreme Court accepted that the words of Article 34 meant that the Article envisaged the future establishment of courts to replace those which existed prior to the adoption of the Constitution of 1937. Such courts were not created until the passing of the Courts (Establishment) Act, 1961 and the Courts (Supplemental Provisions) Act 1961. It followed that the Courts, as established by those Acts, were not bound by decisions of their predecessors.

A final point—which caused some degree of confusion—worthy of mention concerns the various methods of interpretation employed by judges over the years. These mainly fall into two categories—the literal interpretation of the Constitution and the doctrine of harmonious interpretation. The doctrine of harmonious interpretation was elucidated in 1980 by Henchy J. in *Dillane v Ireland*[128], when he said:

> 'Under the doctrine of harmonious interpretation, which requires, where possible, the relevant constitutional provisions to be construed and applied so that each will be given due weight in the circumstances of the case, it would not be a valid form of constitutional interpretation to rule that the

---

125. 1979 IR 73.
126. 1980 IR 32; 113 ILTR 25.
127. 1954 IR 207; 90 ILTR 116.
128. 1980 ILRM 196.

immunity given to a Garda by Rule 67 is necessarily permitted by Article 40.1, and in the same breath to hold that it is proscribed by Article 40.3.2.'

In contrast to this one should examine the case of *The People (The Director of Public Prosecutions) v O'Shea*[129], where the Director of Public Prosecutions sought to appeal an acquittal in the High Court on a criminal charge following a verdict of 'not guilty' by a jury. The Court took literally the meaning of the term 'all' in Article 34.4.3°, which uses the term 'all' when referring to cases which may be appealed from the High Court to the Supreme Court. The Supreme Court decided in favour of the contention by the DPP by a majority of 3:2. Henchy J., dissenting, in support of the doctrine of harmonious interpretation had this to say:

'I agree that if the relevant sub-section of the Constitution is looked at in isolation and is given a literal reading, it would lend itself to that interpretation. But I do not agree that such an approach is a correct method of constitutional interpretation. Any single constitutional right or power is but a component in an ensemble of interconnected and interacting provisions which must be brought into play as part of a larger composition, and which must given such an integrated interpretation as will fit it harmoniously into the general constitutional order and modulation. It may be said of a constitution, more than any other legal instrument, that "the letter killeth, but the spirit giveth life".'

In the later case of *Tormey v Ireland*[130], Henchy J., giving the judgment of the Court, appeared to resolve a certain degree of conflict in this matter when he said:

---

129. 1982 IR 384.
130. 1985 IR 289; 1985 ILRM 375.

'despite its unqualified and unambiguous term the above [i.e. the contrast between sub-sections 4° and 1° of Article 34, section 3] cannot be given an entirely literal construction. The rule of literal interpretation, which is generally applied in the absence of ambiguity or absurdity in the text, must here give way to the more fundamental rule of constitutional interpretation that the Constitution must be read as a whole and that its several provisions must not be looked at in isolation, but be treated as interlocking parts of the general constitutional scheme . . . A judicial attitude of strict construction should be avoided when it would allow the imperfection or inadequacy of the words used to defeat or pervert any of the fundamental purposes of the Constitution.'

It is probably fair to say that this issue is far from resolved.

The stress has been placed somewhat on personal rights by way of illustration, but it should be borne in mind that most aspects of the Constitution have been considered by the courts, over the past twenty-five years in particular, affecting Irish society in major ways. This process continues up to the present and no doubt will continue for so long as the Constitution remains in existence. Huge contributions have been made in the areas of administrative action, fair procedures, education, the family and more recently in controversial areas such as international relations (Crotty's case)[131] and abortion (the 'X' case)[132] and many further areas too numerous to consider here, but which are fully covered in the major textbooks on the subject.

---

131. 1987 IR 713; 1987 ILRM 400.
132. 1992 IR(2) 1; 1992 ILRM 401.

APPENDIX 2

REPORT OF THE COMMITTEE ON THE CONSTITUTION, 1967

In 1966, the three political parties then represented in Dáil Éireann agreed that an informal Committee should be set up 'to review the constitutional, legislative, and institutional bases of Government'.

The Committee was chaired by George Colley, T.D., at that time Minister for Industry and Commerce, and the membership consisted of:

David Andrews, T.D.

Don Davern, T.D.

> (Deputy Davern, on his appointment as Parliamentary Secretary to the Minister for Agriculture, was replaced by Sean F. Lemass, T.D., in November 1966.)

Senator James Dooge

Sean Dunne, T.D.

Denis Jones, T.D.

Robert Molloy, T.D.

Senator Michael O'Kennedy

T. F. O'Higgins, T.D.

Senator Eoin Ryan

Gerard Sweetman, T.D.

James Tully, T.D.

The parties agreed that there would be no obligation to support any recommendations which the Committee might make, even if those recommendations were unanimous. The first meeting of the Committee took place in September 1966 and a total of seventeen meetings took place altogether. During the period for which the Committee deliberated, it received submissions from a number of individuals and bodies and also noted views expressed in various journals as a result of the discussion which arose following the announcement of the setting up of the Committee. The Committee also considered much material relating to foreign constitutions.

At an early stage, it was decided that, where it was not possible to reach unanimity, the substantial arguments for and against each provision of the Constitution under consideration would be set out 'leaving it to the Government of the day to decide the items which should be selected for inclusion in any legislative proposals that might emerge'.

In the introduction to their *Report*, the Committee stated:

> 'we are not aware of any public demand for a change in the basic structure of the Constitution. The republican status of the State, national sovereignty, the supremacy of the people, universal franchise, fundamental rights such as freedom of speech, association and religion, the rule of law and equality before the law, were all part and parcel of this nation's struggle for independence and it is not surprising, perhaps, that, in the minds of the people, they are now to be regarded as virtually unalterable.'

The Committee also considered that there was general acceptance among the majority of the people of the institutions provided by the Constitution and that there was, for example, no apparent desire on the part of any significant group for a departure from the cabinet system of government. Nor did it appear that the people would be prepared to relinquish the requirement that the immediate responsibility of the Government was to Dáil Éireann, being the popularly elected Chamber. The Committee was also of opinion that there was no inclination on the part of the people to invest the Seanad with any greater power than it currently enjoyed. All in all a need was not seen 'to consider any major departure from existing principles'.

While bearing this in mind, the Committee nonetheless considered the matters which were dealt with in their *Report* to be 'of importance for the future good government' of the country and indeed, they expressed the wish that:

> 'every citizen, and particularly every public representative, will analyse carefully the arguments for and against the propositions which we have considered.'

The *Report* was published on 14 December 1967 and consisted of the Committee's consideration of a number of Articles of the Constitution taken in order. This was supplemented by a series of 27 Annexes appended to the main *Report* dealing with a variety of topics.

For the purposes of a work such as this, the authors consider that it is only appropriate to deal (and even then only briefly) with those Articles of the Constitution in respect of which the Committee made definite recommendations based on unanimity. In all other instances the *Report* sets out arguments for and against the particular Article under consideration and it is beyond the scope of this work to consider the arguments propounded other than to refer to the fact that the Committee did not reach unanimity or, where the matter has since been determined by referendum, to refer to that fact.

The *Report* considered Articles 3, 4, 5, 12, 13, 15, 16, 18, 19, 21, 22, 23, 26, 28, 38, 40, 41, 44, 45, 46 and 47 and each of these will be taken in order.

Article 3 — EXTENT OF APPLICATION OF THE LAWS

Article 3 provides as follows:

> 'Pending the re-integration of the national territory, and without prejudice to the right of the Parliament and Government established by this Constitution to

exercise jurisdiction over the whole of that territory, the laws enacted by that Parliament shall have the like area and extent of application as the laws of Saorstát Éireann and the like extra-territorial effect.'

The Committee suggested the substitution of that Article by a new provision, which they suggested should be as follows:

'1. The Irish nation hereby proclaims its firm will that its territory be re-united in harmony and brotherly affection between all Irishmen.

2. The laws enacted by the Parliament established by this Constitution shall, until the achievement of the nation's unity shall otherwise require, have the like area and extent of application as the laws of the Parliament which existed prior to the adoption of this Constitution. Provision may be made by law to give extra-territorial effect to such laws.'

The reason for the final sentence was stated by the Committee to be for the purpose of putting beyond doubt the right of the State to avail of the provisions of the 1958 Geneva Convention on the Continental Shelf in the matter of laws having extra-territorial effect. It also occurred to the Committee that considerations regarding the Continental Shelf might be relevant in relation to Articles 2 and 10 and they recommended appropriate action be taken to rectify the position.

Article 4 — THE NAME OF THE STATE

Article 4 provides as follows:

'The name of the State is Éire, or in the English language, Ireland.'

The Committee were concerned that in the years since 1937 the term 'Éire' had been widely misused in English as the name of the State and they pointed to a certain ambiguity in the Article which could be removed by simply declaring in the English text 'The name of the State is Ireland' and in the Irish text 'Éire is ainm don Stáit'.

Article 5 — REPUBLICAN STATUS AND EXTERNAL FUNCTIONS

This Article states that 'Ireland is a sovereign, independent, democratic state', but neither it nor any other Article proclaims Ireland to be a Republic. The Committee recognised that this omission had been deliberate in 1937. The Republic of Ireland Act, 1948 declared the description of the State to be the Republic of Ireland. This Act also repealed the Executive Authority (External Relations) Act, 1936 and conferred on the President the necessary powers and functions of the State in connection with external affairs—such powers and functions being previously exercised by the British Monarch. The Committee considered that, as the State was a Republic and recognised internationally as such, it was desirable to amend Article 5 so as to provide that the State is a sovereign, independent, democratic Republic. The Committee stated that this would achieve the same objective as section 2 of the Republic of Ireland Act, 1948.

Continuing with their treatment of the Act of 1948, the Committee referred to section 3, which contains a declaration that the President may exercise the executive power of the State in relation to foreign affairs (which the Committee pointed out is 'in pursuance of the Powers given under Article 28.2 which provides that the executive power of the State will be exercised by or on the authority of the Government'), and they also referred to the repeal by section 1 of the 1948 Act of the Executive Authority (External Relations) Act, 1936. The Committee considered that Article 12 of the Constitution should be amended 'in order to complete the tidying up process' and suggested the replacement of Article 12.1 as follows:

'Article 12

1. 1° There shall be a President of Ireland (Uachtarán na hÉireann) who shall take precedence over all other persons in the State.

2° The President may exercise the executive power of the State or any executive function of the State only on the advice of the Government and shall exercise and perform the other powers and functions conferred on the President by this Constitution and by law.'

Article 12.1 — THE OFFICE OF PRESIDENT

The Committee considered a proposal that the separate office of President be abolished and set out in their *Report* the arguments adduced for and against.

Article 12.2 — METHOD OF ELECTING THE PRESIDENT

The Committee considered a proposal that the President should be elected by an electoral college and set out in their *Report* the arguments adduced for and against. In addition, in Annex 1 of the *Report*, information was given in regard to the President's functions under the Constitution and also in regard to the methods of election adopted in other countries.

Article 12.4 — NOMINATION FOR PRESIDENTIAL ELECTION

Article 12.4.2 of the Constitution provides that a candidate for election of President, *other than a former or retiring President*, must be nominated by no less than twenty members of the Oireachtas, or by the Councils of not less than four administrative counties. Article 12.4.4 provides that former or retiring Presidents may become candidates on their own nomination. The Committee were of the view that sub-section 4 of Article 12.4 should be deleted, recognising that this would give rise to a consequential change in sub-section 2 of Article 12.4.

Article 13.1 — SELECTION OF TAOISEACH

Article 13.1 of the Constitution provides that the President shall, on the nomination of the Dáil, appoint the Taoiseach. The Committee considered the question of 'making some change' in the requirement that the Taoiseach can only be appointed on the nomination of the Dáil. They '. . . took note of the provisions of other Constitutions in this respect' and Annex 2 of the *Report* contains an extract from the Inter-Parliamentary Union publication *Parliaments* (1966) which gives a summary of the general situation of Heads of Government in 55 countries covered by an Inter-Parliamentary Union survey.

In view of the possibility that a situation could arise at some stage in the future where no party leader would be able to secure nomination by a Dáil majority, the Committee considered the 'introduction of an arrangement involving the granting of discretionary powers to the Head of State in this connection'. The arrangement would be to the effect that the President would — either after a general election or on the relinquishment of office by a Taoiseach—'designate to be Taoiseach the member of the Dáil whom he considered most likely to secure the confidence of the House, and appoint Ministers on his nomination, these appointments to remain effective until there is a vote of no confidence in the Dáil.' The Committee stated the main purpose of this change would be 'to eliminate the danger of the country being without effective Government for a lengthy period while different candidates strove for a majority in the Dáil.'

The Committee set out in their *Report* the arguments adduced for and against the proposal.

In this section of the *Report*, the Committee also referred to Article 28.11 of the Constitution, under which it is provided that the members of the Government in office at the date of dissolution of Dáil Éireann shall continue to hold office until their successors have been appointed. The Committee were of opinion that, notwithstanding the provisions of Section 7 of that Article, this seemed to enable the outgoing Government to continue even though some of its members might have lost their seats in a general election. The Committee referred to the fact that 'the Taoiseach of such a Government would also seem to have the same right as an ordinary Taoiseach in the matter of seeking a dissolution, etc.'

The Committee gave some attention to the provisions relating to the continuance in office of the old Government, should the new Dáil fail to appoint a new Government. It agreed that it might be desirable to provide for the previous Government to remain in office while attempts were being made to appoint a successor. The Committee decided that, for a period of a few months, such a Government should not have the right to seek a dissolution without an order of the House, and that, in the event of failure to appoint a Government within that period, a further general election would have to be held. The Committee also considered that the situation which could arise where the Taoiseach resigned without a dissolution would also have to be examined. They were also of the opinion that powers might have to be granted to the President to ensure adherence to these provisions.

Article 13.2.3 — POWER OF PRESIDENT TO CONVENE MEETINGS OF HOUSES OF THE OIREACHTAS

Under this Article, the President has the power, after consultation with the Council of State, to convene a meeting of either or both Houses of the Oireachtas. The Committee recommended that this provision should be extended to further provide that 'a specified number of members of the Oireachtas should have the right to require the President to convene a meeting of either or both Houses.'

Article 15.10 — PARLIAMENTARY PRIVILEGE

Article 15.10 provides as follows:

> 'Each House shall make its own rules and standing orders, with power to attach penalties for their infringement, and shall have power to ensure freedom of debate, to protect its official documents and the private papers of its members, and to protect itself and its members against any person or persons interfering with, molesting or attempting to corrupt its members in the exercise of their duties.'

Having considered the Article, the Committee came to the conclusion that it

> 'ought to be regarded as empowering the Houses of the Oireachtas to deal with internal matters of procedure and discipline only, and to punish its own members for breaches of its rules; it should, of course, also be open to each House to withdraw any privileges from any such persons as transgress any regulations of the House. In addition, each House should have the power to deal effectively with persons who endeavour to disrupt its proceedings. All other offences against Parliament and its members should, in our view, be

dealt with by a special Act of the Oireachtas on the same lines as the legislation passed by other countries. If so desired, the Chairman of each House could be empowered to make complaints to the Attorney General requesting that particular matters be investigated with a view to prosecution. If amendment of Article 15.10 is required to enable these matters to be dealt with in this way, then we recommend that the change should be made.'

The Committee considered, at some length, the advantages of the recommendation and set out further information in Annex 3 to the *Report*.

Article 16.1.2 — QUALIFYING AGE FOR VOTING

The Committee considered two alternatives only (21 years, as the qualifying age then was, and 18 years, as proposed in a submission to the Committee) and the *Report* sets out the arguments adduced for and against the proposal. This matter has since been determined by the Fourth Amendment of the Constitution in 1972, which provided for the reduction of the qualifying age to 18.

Article 16.2.2 — NUMBER OF PERSONS PER MEMBER OF PARLIAMENT

This Article provides that the total number of Dáil members shall not be less than one member for each 30,000 of the population, or more than one member for each 20,000. The Committee gave 'some consideration to the question of enlarging the membership of Dáil Éireann'. In Annex 5 to their *Report*, the Committee provided information about the situation as it then was in other countries, and in the body of the *Report* they set out the arguments adduced in favour of and against an increase in the number of Deputies in Dáil Éireann. The Committee, while admitting a divergence of views on a proposal immediately to increase the size of the Dail, felt that the upper limit of 30,000 as laid down in Article 16.2.2 had 'lost its significance' in light of the fact that the practice of the Oireachtas in dealing with constituency matters had been to adhere as closely as possible to the lower limit of 20,000 persons (further information on this point being provided in Annex 10 to the *Report*). The Committee thought that 'a more realistic tolerance would be the range 22,500–17,500 persons' and recommended amendment accordingly.

Article 16.2.3 — DELIMITATION OF CONSTITUENCIES

This Article provides that the ratio between the number of members to be elected for each constituency and the population of each constituency shall, so far as it is practicable, be the same throughout the country. In 1959 the constituencies had been revised following the 1956 census, which had shown changes in population which necessitated revision in accordance with Article 16.2.4, and applying Article 16.2.3.

Here the Committee referred to the case of *O'Donovan v The Attorney General*[133] in which the High Court had found that statutory provisions contained in the Electoral (Amendment), 1959 were unconstitutional (Annex 6 to the *Report* reproduces some relevant extracts from the decision of the High Court in that case). The Committee particularly noted that the Court had found:

'there was no indication in the Constitution that it was intended that any of the difficulties as to the working of the parliamentary system should be taken into consideration on the question of practicability and that the difficulties to which the legislature should have regard are those of an administrative and statistical nature.'

---

133. 1961 IR 114; 96 ILRM 121.

The Committee also considered the 'problem of rural representation' which had arisen in other countries with a declining rural population and this topic is further covered in Annexes 7 and 8 of the *Report*.

The *Report* set down arguments adduced in favour of and against a change in the system.

Article 16.2.5 — THE ELECTORAL SYSTEM: THE PRESENT SYSTEM, ITS ORIGIN AND RESULTS.

The *Report* here referred to Article 16.2.5 (which provides for the use of the system of proportional representation by means of the single transferable vote) and outlined the operation of the system. Annex 9 of the *Report* provided information on the history of the proportional representation system in Ireland and Annex 10 gave information about the size of constituencies, number of Dáil members and total population throughout the years (up to the mid-1960s). Annexes 11 to 15 provided other information on the workings of the system.

The Committee considered the question of adopting a different electoral system for Dáil elections. The substitution of the proportional representation system by the Alternative Vote was the subject of a proposal and the *Report* sets out the arguments adduced for and against this proposal.

Articles 18 and 19 — THE SEANAD

Annexes 18 to 23 of the *Report* set out the history of Seanad Éireann together with information about the existing Constitutional and statutory provisions in relation to its composition, powers and various other matters.

While the opinion of the Committee was generally in favour of a second House of the Oireachtas it nonetheless set out in the *Report* arguments adduced in favour of and against the retention of the Seanad. The Committee also referred to the fact that the Constitution allows 'extreme flexibility' in relation to the Seanad and suggested that ordinary legislation could bring about fundamental changes in relation to it. They did not 'feel obliged to consider each and every existing provision relating to the Seanad' since they were primarily concerned with the Constitution. Nonetheless, they considered various possibilities which they stated to be for the purpose of meeting criticisms 'which have been expressed from time to time in relation to the Seanad' and they summarised their views under various headings:

THE VOCATIONAL AND FUNCTIONAL PRINCIPLE—the Committee were of the view that the principle of a second chamber composed on vocational or functional lines should be preserved, and that the need for Constitutional amendment had not been proved, having regard especially, it would seem, to the possibilities of reform by means of ordinary legislation.

GEOGRAPHICAL COMPOSITION AND METHOD OF ELECTION—the Committee considered a variety of proposals in relation to the 'geographical composition of the Seanad' and they set out a number of points which they had considered in this regard. The Report states the Committee to be opposed, in general, to the 'idea of direct elections of Senators by the people'.

TERM OF OFFICE—the Committee rejected the idea of a system which allowed for the vacation of only half of the Seanad seats on the dissolution of the Dáil, doing so on the basis that while it might contribute to the stability which is often regarded as a desirable feature of a second chamber, they saw a danger in that the personnel of the Seanad might not 'adequately reflect changes in public opinion which would be represented to a fuller extent in the more recently elected popular chamber'. They also saw the further danger that such a situation could 'give rise to a situation in which the two houses of the legislature find themselves at loggerheads'.

ELECTION OF NOMINATING BODIES' CANDIDATES—the Committee placed on record their view 'that further consideration might now be given to the possibility of increasing the minimum representation attainable by the candidates put forward on behalf of nominating bodies'.

DIRECT ELECTION BY NOMINATING BODIES—the Committee were unanimous in the view that all suggestions to this effect should be rejected, as this would lead to a situation where political parties would take a greater interest in the internal affairs of Nominating Bodies. This should be avoided 'at all costs'.

UNIVERSITY SENATORS—the Committee set down the arguments adduced for and against university representation. Circumstances have been changed by the Fourth Amendment of the Constitution Act, 1972.

POWERS OF THE SEANAD—the Committee doubted if there was any substantial number of persons who would wish to see the powers of the Seanad increased.

Article 21 *et seq.* — DISTINCTIONS BETWEEN DIFFERENT KINDS OF BILLS

Annex 24 of the *Report* contained information in connection with provisions relating to different kinds of Bills under Articles 21, 23, 24, 26 and 27.

The Committee stated that it was clear that in the case of a Money Bill, Articles 23, 26 and 27 did not apply. They were unanimously of the view that it was necessary to 'place Money Bills in this unique position' and pointed to the fact that the need to give the Dáil special powers in relation to financial matters had been recognised since the inception of the State. They felt it necessary to point out also that the constitutionality of a Money Bill could be contested in the Courts under the provisions of Article 34.3.2 in the ordinary way. On this basis they felt that there should be no change in relation to Bills passed under Article 24.

Article 23.1 — DÁIL RESOLUTION DEEMING BILLS TO HAVE BEEN PASSED BY BOTH HOUSES

This Article enables the Dáil to limit to 90 days the amount of time available to the Seanad for consideration of ordinary Bills. After the expiry of this period, the Dáil may resolve that the Bill is deemed to have been passed by both Houses, but such a resolution must be passed within 180 days of the day it was sent by the Dáil to the Seanad. The Committee felt that it would be desirable:

> 'to amplify Article 23 so as to provide that the resolution passed by the Dáil may specify the amendments passed by the Seanad which are to be made in the Bill and that the Bill so amended shall, subject to any further Dáil amendments arising out of the Seanad amendments, be the one which is deemed to have passed both Houses.'

Article 26 — REFERENCE OF BILLS TO THE SUPREME COURT BY THE PRESIDENT

The Committee, while unanimous in their view that Article 26 should be retained, felt that some changes were necessary, but stated they were 'unable to agree on the best approach to the problem'.

With regard to Article 34.3.3, the Committee referred to the view that an enactment should be capable of being challenged at any time and said that this view suggests that such an approach 'would be justifiable in view of the abandonment of *stare decisis* for ordinary proceedings including constitutional proceedings for constitutional validity under Article 34.' This argument, if accepted, suggests that the Supreme Court should have equal freedom in the case of decisions under Article 26 and acceptance of such a proposal would involve the deletion of Article 34.3.3. Such deletion would negate the object of Article 26. An alternative suggestion would be that the existing provisions be amended so as to allow a Supreme Court decision under Article 26 to be challenged in further legal proceedings after a period of, for example, seven years.

Under the provisions of Article 26.2.2 and Article 34.4.5, the decision of the Supreme Court on the constitutionality of a Bill or law must take the form of one judgment. The Committee felt that any change which would allow the publication of minority opinions dissenting from the majority judgment would 'only tend to create uncertainty in the minds of the people on matters of constitutional importance'.

Under Article 26.3.1, where the Supreme Court decides that any provision of a Bill is repugnant to the Constitution, the President must decline to sign the entire Bill. In this regard the Committee had considered a suggestion that where only part of a Bill was found to be invalid by the Supreme Court, the remainder might be signed by the President. The Committee were of opinion that this provision should not be amended and that the best course of action would be to have the Bill re-drafted and re-submitted to the Oireachtas in an acceptable form.

Article 28 — EMERGENCY POWERS

The *Report* considered the question of the Constitutional Amendments of 1939 and 1941 and the resolution in 1939 by each House of the Oireachtas that a state of national emergency existed. Having arrived at the view that the determination of the existence of a state of national emergency or otherwise was a political determination (and therefore judicial examination of the question was inappropriate), the Committee were of opinion that the time had come to devise a formula which would 'answer in some way the complaints which have been made against the continuance in effect of the relevant provisions'. The Committee recommended that consideration be given to the question of adding to Article 28.3.3 a clause providing that resolutions declaring an emergency shall have effect for a period of three years only unless renewed by further resolutions of the Dáil and Seanad.

The Committee also referred to the expression 'in the case of actual invasion' contained in Article 28.3.2. They viewed this expression as being no longer appropriate in view of developments in long-range warfare and recommended that an amendment should be introduced:

> 'to cover also apprehended attack by unmanned missiles or other modern weapons which might not necessarily involve the presence of human enemies on the national territory.'

Article 38 — SPECIAL CRIMINAL COURTS

The Committee's examination of this matter has largely been overtaken by later developments. It is interesting to note, however, that the Committee did not recommend any constitutional restrictions in regard to the use of persons unqualified in the law (e.g. army officers) as opposed to members of the judiciary. The present Special Criminal Court, in existence since 1972, is made up solely of members of the judiciary and it is difficult to envisage a departure from this state of affairs in the current political and social climate.

Article 40.4.1 — RESTRICTIONS ON PERSONAL LIBERTY

This Article provides that no citizen may be deprived of his personal liberty save in accordance with law and the Committee examined the expression 'save in accordance with law'.

The Committee referred to the decisions in the cases of *Ryan v The Attorney General*[134] *and Macauly v The Minister for Posts and Telegraphs*[135] which showed, in their opinion, that:

> 'the Supreme Court which upheld the Offences Against the State Bill in 1940[136] [in that case the Supreme Court held the Offences Against the State Bill to be consistent with the Constitution] may now be prepared to adopt, towards the expression in question, an attitude different from that which influenced it in the case of the Offences Against The State Bill and other proceedings.'

Accordingly, no amendment was recommended.

The *Report* also referred to the fact that the Supreme Court by virtue of the Courts (Establishment and Constitution) Act, 1961, was no longer bound by decisions of the pre-1961 Supreme Court and therefore, 'the judicial determination of such vital questions as fundamental rights can be reviewed from time to time in the light of changing circumstances'. The *Report* goes on to state:

> '[In this particular instance] we are satisfied that a solution to the problem we are discussing can only be found by judicial decision since we see no hope of devising suitable constitutional provisions which would guarantee the right to personal liberty and at the same time indicate in detail the circumstances in which it can be denied by law.'

---

134. 1965 IR 294.
135. 1966 IR 345.
136. 1940 IR 470; 74 ILT 61.

Article 40 — TRADE UNION ISSUES

The matters discussed under the heading of this Article have since been addressed by legislation and any discussion on the points considered by the Committee, while relevant in 1966/7, cannot be said to have very much relevance today.

In any case the Committee did not recommend any constitutional changes in this area.

Articles 41.3 and 44.2 — PROVISIONS RELATING TO MARRIAGE

At the outset the Committee appeared to be concerned with the prohibition against the dissolution of marriage contained in Article 41.3.2 as being 'an embarrassment to those seeking to bring about better relations between North and South since the majority of the Northern population have divorce rights under the law applicable to that area'. Reference was made in the *Report* to the fact that other predominantly Catholic countries do not absolutely prohibit divorce and reference was also made to 'the more liberal attitude prevailing in Catholic circles in regard to the rites and practices of other religious denominations, particularly since the Second Vatican Council'. On this basis, the Committee felt that the object underlying the prohibition contained in the Article (the *Report* did not suggest the precise nature of this object) could be better achieved by the use of wording which would 'not give offence to any of the religions professed by the inhabitants of this country'. They recommended a provision along the following lines which they felt would 'meet the wishes of Catholics and non-Catholics alike':

> 'In the case of a person who was married in accordance with the rites of a religion, no law shall be enacted providing for the grant of a dissolution of that marriage on grounds other than those acceptable to that religion.'

The Committee viewed the absolute prohibition contained in the Constitution as being coercive in relation to both Catholics and non-Catholics alike and pointed to the fact that the Catholic Church permitted the dissolution of marriages in certain circumstances, while the prohibition contained in Article 41 had the effect of imposing on Catholics 'regulations more rigid than those required by the law of the Church'.

The *Report* went on to consider Article 41.3.3 and stated that if Article 41.3.2 were amended as suggested, 'it would be necessary to look again at the provisions of sub-section 3'. They accepted that the words of sub-section 3 created some difficulties in 1937 and had been the cause of 'some confusion' since. Having looked at some case law—*M.P. v M.P.* (1958 IR 336) and the English decision in *B. v B.* (1961 3 All ER 225)—and the findings of a working party on the provision drawn from the Office of the Attorney General and from the Department of External Affairs in 1940, the Committee were 'drawn to the conclusion' that the sub-section should be deleted entirely. This matter has since been dealt with by the legislature to a degree by the passing of the Domicile and Recognition of Foreign Divorces Act, 1986 (Number 24 of 1986).

The Committee also considered Article 44.2.3 which provides that:

> 'The State shall not impose any disabilities or make any discrimination on the ground of religious profession, belief or status.'

This Article was considered in light of the Marriage Acts which provide that different conditions are to apply to marriages performed in accordance with the rites of the Church of Ireland, the Presbyterian Church, other Protestant Churches and the Jewish Religion. The Committee referred to an opinion which considered that the provisions contained in the Marriage Acts constituted discrimination within the meaning of Article 44.2.3 and recommended that any difficulty could be removed by adding a suitable provision to the effect that the prohibition on religious discrimination should not prevent the 'enactment of different procedural rules relating to different kinds of marriage ceremonies with a view to ensuring that all legal rules are complied with by the parties concerned'. The Committee's concern here related to their view that some of the smaller denominations were not sufficiently organised to ensure that parties who presented themselves for marriage were, in fact, free to marry. They did not consider the abolition of the conditions relating to the marriage of non-Catholics to be an 'advisable step'.

Article 42.3.2 — SCHOOL ATTENDANCE

Here, having considered the Supreme Court decision in the Article 26 Reference of the School Attendance Bill in 1943 (1943 IR 334), and being of opinion that conditions had changed since 1943, the Committee suggested that Article 42.3.2 might be replaced by a provision which they suggested could be along the following lines:

> '2. Laws, however, may be enacted to oblige parents who have failed in their duty to provide for the education of their children to send their children to schools established or designated by the State.'

The Committee further stated that in putting forward this suggestion, they did not wish to infringe the rights of parents under Article 42.2.

Article 44.1 — RECOGNITION OF RELIGIONS

The recommendations of the Committee were carried out by the Fifth Amendment of the Constitution in 1972.

Article 45 — DIRECTIVE PRINCIPLES OF SOCIAL POLICY

Here, the Committee expressed the view that the Article should include a provision establishing the principle of equal pay for men and women for work of equal value.

Articles 46 and 47 — AMENDMENT OF THE CONSTITUTION

Article 46 provides that the Constitution can be changed only by referendum.

The Committee examined various formulae which might be adopted for the purpose of permitting constitutional changes to be brought about while 'at the same time maintaining the essential supremacy of the Constitution over ordinary law'. On this subject, further information was given in Annex 25 of the *Report*.

The Committee considered a proposal 'for some relaxation of the rigid rule laid down in Article 46' and set down the arguments adduced for and against such a relaxation.

The Committee also referred to the fact that under Article 47 a proposal for the amendment of the Constitution required a mere majority of votes cast in a referendum for its approval, and considered whether any safeguard should be introduced to deal with a situation where only a small percentage of the electorate actually voted. On balance, the Committee did not feel any change was necessary here.

Spent Matter

Finally, the Committee referred to the fact that they had observed a number of matters (which they did not consider necessary to list) which were, by 1967, obviously spent and felt that, wherever possible, the opportunity should be taken to remove them from the Constitution.

GENERAL COMMENT

From the tenor of the 1967 *Report*, it appears clear that the Committee did not perceive any fundamental flaw in the Constitution of 1937. In most respects, the *Report* reflects a desire to let sleeping dogs lie and displays no great wish to interfere with institutions which they viewed as adequate. At the same time, it does reflect a mood of reconciliation with Northern Ireland.

In regard to the conservatism of the *Report*, it will be noted that even the recommendations on matters such as the dissolution of marriage were framed in such a manner as to avoid any question of making divorce available to members of the majority Church and indeed, the formula suggested in the *Report* would, quite possibly, have been capable of surviving the scrutiny of all but the most conservative elements of Irish society in 1967.

APPENDIX 3

CHRONOLOGY

1922	
25 October	The Constitution of the Irish Free State (Saorstát Éireann) Act, 1922, embodying the Constitution, enacted by Dáil Éireann.
1935	
30 April/ 2 May	de Valera instructs John Hearne, legal adviser in the Department of External Affairs, to prepare draft heads for a new Constitution.
18 May	Hearne submits draft heads.
1936	
5 June	Executive Council authorises the President to inform Edward VIII of the intention of the Irish government to introduce a Bill for the purpose of setting up a new Constitution.
8 June	Irish High Commissioner in London delivers a memo to Edward VIII outlining the intentions of the Irish government.
1937	
10 March	Draft Constitution Bill introduced in Dáil.
12 March	Executive Council agrees to treat Draft Constitution as a Bill.
16 March	Confidential distribution of first draft without the Article on religion.

1 April	First revision completed and printed.
10 April	Preamble in final form, second revision circulated.
16 April	Joseph Walshe, Secretary of the Department of External Affairs, sent to Vatican to seek Papal approval for Draft Constitution.
22 April	Walshe reports Vatican acquiescence.
23 April	Third revision completed.
27 April	Executive Council discusses complete text and the printers are ordered to print 1,200 copies for distribution to clergy, judiciary, Dáil, and prominent public figures abroad.
1 May	Constitution published and circulated.
11/13 May	Second Reading in Dáil.
17 May	*Irish Press* reports praise for Constitution published by *Osservatore Romano*.
25 May/ 3 June	Third Reading (Committee Stage).
14 June	Approved by Dáil Éireann (unicameral Oireachtas).
1 July	Constitution of Ireland enacted by the people [referendum]; general election held; de Valera returned.
29 December	Date of coming into operation of the Constitution.

1938	
31 January	Copy of the Constitution is certified by the Clerk of the Dáil (Art. 63).
16 February	Copy of the Constitution signed by the Taoiseach (Eamon de Valera), the Chief Justice (Timothy Sullivan) and the Chairman of Dáil Éireann.
18 February	Copy of Constitution enrolled in the Office of the Registrar of the Supreme Court.
27 April	Seanad meets for the first time.
4 May	President elected.
27 May	Dáil dissolved.
25 June	President entered office.
30 June	General election—de Valera returned.
1939	
2 September	All stages of the First Amendment of the Constitution Bill, 1939 pass in both the Dáil and the Seanad, and the Bill is signed by the President.
1940	
27 November	Second Amendment of the Constitution Bill, 1940: introduced in Dáil Éireann.
1941	
2 April	Second Amendment of the Constitution Bill, 1940: Dáil Committee Stage.

24 April	Second Amendment of the Constitution Bill, 1940: Committee Stage passed by the Dáil.
7 May	Second Amendment of the Constitution Bill, 1940: declared carried by the Dáil.
14 May	Second Amendment of the Constitution Bill, 1940: introduced in the Seanad.
21 May	Second Amendment of the Constitution Bill, 1940: Seanad Committee Stage.
27 May	Second Amendment of the Constitution Bill, 1940: Seanad Report and Final Stages.
30 May	Second Amendment of the Constitution Act, 1940: signed by the President.
1942	
25 March	The text of the Constitution of Ireland as amended by the first two Acts to amend the Constitution prepared in accordance with Article 25 is enrolled in the Office of the Registrar of the Supreme Court.
1959	
19 March	Seanad rejects the Third Amendment of the Constitution Bill, 1958.
13 May	Dáil deems the Third Amendment of the Constitution Bill, 1958, to be passed.
17 June	Referendum on the Third Amendment of the Constitution Bill, 1958. [Referendum to abolish proportional representation, defeated by 453,322 votes to 486,989.]

1968	
16 October	Referenda on the Third Amendment of the Constitution Bill, 1968, and on the Fourth Amendment of the Constitution Bill, 1968. [The former to allow a 16 % variation in the proportion of population per T.D., defeated by 424,185 votes to 656,803; the latter to introduce the straight vote, defeated by 423,496 votes to 657,898.]
1971	
23 November	Third Amendment of the Constitution Bill, 1971: introduced in Dáil Éireann.
2 December	Third Amendment of the Constitution Bill, 1971: Dáil Second Stage.
9 December	Third Amendment of the Constitution Bill, 1971: Second Stage passed by the Dáil.
1972	
25 January	Third Amendment of the Constitution Bill, 1971: Dáil Committee Stage.
26 January	Third Amendment of the Constitution Bill, 1971: declared carried by Dáil Éireann.
24 February	Third Amendment of the Constitution Bill, 1971: Second stage introduced in the Seanad.
1 March	Third Amendment of the Constitution Bill, 1971: Seanad Committee Stage.

8 March	Third Amendment of the Constitution Bill, 1971: Seanad Report and Final Stages.
10 May	Referendum on the Third Amendment of the Constitution Bill, 1971, carried.
8 June	Third Amendment of the Constitution Act, 1972: signed by the President.
28 June	Fourth Amendment of the Constitution Bill, 1972: introduced in the Dáil.
5 July	Fourth Amendment of the Constitution Bill, 1972: Dáil Second Stage introduced and passed.
11 July	Fourth Amendment of the Constitution Bill, 1972: Dáil Third, Fourth and Fifth Stages passed.
13 July	Fourth Amendment of the Constitution Bill, 1972: Second and subsequent Stages in the Seanad.
26 October	Fifth Amendment of the Constitution Bill, 1972: Dáil First Stage.
2 November	Fifth Amendment of the Constitution Bill, 1972: Dáil Second and subsequent Stages.
3 November	Fifth Amendment of the Constitution Bill, 1972: all Stages passed in the Seanad.
7 December	Referenda on the Fourth Amendment of the Constitution Bill, 1972, and the Fifth Amendment of the Constitution Bill, 1972. Both carried.

1973	
5 January	Fifth Amendment of the Constitution Act, 1972 and Fourth Amendment of the Constitution Act, 1972: signed by the President.
1978	
13 December	Sixth Amendment of the Constitution (Adoption) Bill, 1978: introduced in Dáil Éireann.
1979	
7 February	Sixth Amendment of the Constitution (Adoption) Bill, 1978: Dáil Second Stage.
14 February	Sixth Amendment of the Constitution (Adoption) Bill, 1978: Dáil Second Stage resumed.
28 February	Sixth Amendment of the Constitution (Adoption) Bill, 1978: Dáil Committee and Final Stages.
7 March	Sixth Amendment of the Constitution (Adoption) Bill, 1978: introduced in Seanad Éireann.
28 March	Sixth Amendment of the Constitution (Adoption) Bill 1978: Seanad Committee Stage passed without amendment.
5 April	Seanad Report and Final Stages passed.

3 May	Seventh Amendment of the Constitution (Election of Members of Seanad Éireann by Institutions of Higher Education) Bill, 1979: introduced in Dáil Éireann.
22 May	Seventh Amendment of the Constitution (Election of Members of Seanad Éireann by Institutions of Higher Education) Bill, 1979: Dáil Second Stage.
23 May	Seventh Amendment of the Constitution (Election of Members of Seanad Éireann by Institutions of Higher Education) Bill, 1979: Dáil Committee and subsequent Stages passed.
31 May	Seventh Amendment of the Constitution (Election of Members of Seanad Éireann by Institutions of Higher Education) Bill, 1979: introduced in the Seanad, all stages passed.
5 July	Referendum on the Sixth Amendment of the Constitution (Adoption) Bill, 1978, carried. Referendum on the Seventh Amendment of the Constitution (Election of Members of Seanad Éireann by Institutions of Higher Education) Bill, 1979, carried.
3 August	Sixth Amendment of the Constitution (Adoption) Act, 1979: signed by the President. Seventh Amendment of the Constitution (Election of Members of Seanad Éireann by Institutions of Higher Education) Act, 1979: signed by the President.

2 November	Eighth Amendment of the Constitution Bill, 1982: introduced in the Dáil.
1983	
2 February	Eighth Amendment of the Constitution Bill, 1982: restored to the Dáil Order Paper following the general election.
9 February	Eighth Amendment of the Constitution, 1982: Dáil Second Stage.
17 February	Eighth Amendment of the Constitution Bill, 1982: Dáil Second Stage resumed.
23 February	Eighth Amendment of the Constitution Bill, 1982: Dáil Second Stage resumed.
2 March	Eighth Amendment of the Constitution Bill, 1982: Dáil Second Stage resumed.
8 March	Eighth Amendment of the Constitution Bill, 1982: Dáil Second Stage resumed.
24 March	Eighth Amendment of the Constitution Bill, 1982: Dáil Second Stage passed.
27 April	Eighth Amendment of the Constitution Bill, 1982: Dáil Committee and subsequent Stages passed.
4 May	Eighth Amendment of the Constitution Bill, 1982: introduced in Seanad Éireann (Second Stage).
5 May	Eighth Amendment of the Constitution Bill, 1982: Seanad Second Stage resumed.

11 May	Eighth Amendment of the Constitution Bill, 1982: Seanad Second Stage passed.
18 May	Eighth Amendment of the Constitution Bill, 1982: Seanad Committee Stage.
19 May	Eighth Amendment of the Constitution Bill, 1982: Seanad Committee Stage passed without amendment.
25 May	Eighth Amendment of the Constitution Bill, 1982: Seanad Report Stage.
26 May	Eighth Amendment of the Constitution Bill, 1982: Seanad Report Stage resumed and Bill passed all Stages.
7 September	Referendum on the Eighth Amendment of the Constitution Bill, 1982, carried.
7 October	Eighth Amendment of the Constitution Act, 1983: signed by the President.
1984	
5 April	Ninth Amendment of the Constitution Bill, 1984: introduced in Dáil Éireann.
11 April	Ninth Amendment of the Constitution Bill, 1984: Second Stage introduced in Dáil Éireann and passed all Stages. Introduced in Seanad Éireann and passed all Stages.
14 June	Referendum on the Ninth Amendment of the Constitution Bill, 1984, carried.
2 August	Ninth Amendment of the Constitution Act, 1984: signed by the President.

1986	
26 June	Referendum on the Tenth Amendment of the Constitution Bill, 1986, to provide for the dissolution of marriage. The Bill was defeated by 538,279 votes to 935,843.

1987	
22 April	Tenth Amendment of the Constitution Bill, 1987: introduced in the Dáil.
23 April	Tenth Amendment of the Constitution Bill, 1987: Second Stage carried.
24 April	Tenth Amendment of the Constitution Bill, 1987: Committee and subsequent Stages carried.
25 April	Tenth Amendment of the Constitution Bill, 1987: introduced in the Seanad and passed all stages without amendment.
26 May	Referendum on the Tenth Amendment of the Constitution Bill, 1987: to allow ratification of the Single European Act, carried.
22 June	Tenth Amendment of the Constitution Act, 1987: signed by the President.

1989	
15 December	Agreement relating to Community Patents (drawn up between the Member States of the Communities and done at Luxembourg on the 15th day of December, 1989) is signed.

1992	
7 February	Treaty on European Union signed at Maastricht, The Netherlands.
5 May	Eleventh Amendment of the Constitution Bill, 1992: Dáil Second Stage.
6 May	Eleventh Amendment of the Constitution Bill, 1992: Second Stage resumed.
7 May	Eleventh Amendment of the Constitution Bill, 1992: Dáil Second Stage resumed and passed; Committee and subsequent Stages passed.
14 May	Eleventh Amendment of the Constitution Bill, 1992: Seanad Second Stage.
15 May	Eleventh Amendment of the Constitution Bill, 1992: Seanad Second Stage resumed; Second and all subsequent Stages passed.
18 June	Referendum on the Eleventh Amendment of the Constitution Bill, 1992, passed.
16 July	Eleventh Amendment of the Constitution Act, 1992: signed by the President.
20 October	Twelfth Amendment of the Constitution Bill, 1992: Dáil Second Stage. This Bill proposed to amend the Constitution by the addition—in sub-section 3° of section 3 of Article 40 of the English text—immediately after the words 'vindicate that right' of the words 'It shall be unlawful to terminate the life of an unborn unless such termination is necessary to save the life, as distinct from the health, of

	the mother where there is an illness or disorder of the mother giving rise to a real and substantial risk to her life, not being a risk of self-destruction'.
21 October	Twelfth Amendment of the Constitution Bill, 1992: Dáil Second Stage resumed and, unusually, ran over midnight.
22 October	Thirteenth Amendment of the Constitution Bill, 1992: Dáil Second Stage commenced between midnight and one o'clock in the morning. Fourteenth Amendment of the Constitution Bill, 1992: Dáil Second Stage passed. The Dáil Committee Stage was taken between 12.00 and 1.00 a.m. All stages passed. Thirteenth Amendment of the Constitution Bill, 1992: Dáil Committee and subsequent Stages taken later in the morning, shortly after 10.30 a.m. All stages passed. Twelfth Amendment of the Constitution Bill, 1992: Dáil Second Stage resumed and passed without amendment.
27 October	Twelfth Amendment of the Constitution Bill, 1992: Dáil Committee and subsequent Stages passed.
28 October	Twelfth Amendment of the Constitution Bill, 1992: Seanad Second Stage.
29 October	Twelfth Amendment of the Constitution Bill, 1992: Seanad Second Stage resumed. Thirteenth Amendment of the Constitution Bill, 1992: Seanad Second Stage passed.

	Fourteenth Amendment of the Constitution Bill, 1992: Seanad Second Stage passed.
30 October	Twelfth Amendment of the Constitution Bill, 1992: Seanad Committee and subsequent Stages passed.
	Thirteenth Amendment of the Constitution Bill, 1992: Seanad Committee and subsequent Stages passed.
	Fourteenth Amendment of the Constitution Bill, 1992: Seanad Committee and subsequent Stages passed.
25 November	Referenda on the Twelfth, Thirteenth and Fourteenth Amendment of the Constitution Bills, 1992. The Twelfth Amendment of the Constitution Bill, 1992, was not passed. The Thirteenth and Fourteenth Amendment of the Constitution Bills were carried.
23 December	Thirteenth Amendment of the Constitution Act, 1992, and Fourteenth Amendment of the Constitution Act, 1992: signed by the President.

FURTHER READING

BOOKS

Casey, James, *Constitutional Law in Ireland,* London: Sweet & Maxwell 1987.

Chubb, Basil, *The Constitution and Constitutional Change in Ireland,* Dublin: I.P.A. 1978.

Chubb, Basil, *The Politics of the Irish Constitution,* Dublin: I.P.A. 1987.

Doolan, Brian, *Constitutional Law and Constitutional Rights in Ireland,* 2nd ed., Dublin: Gill & Macmillan 1988.

Farrell, Brian (ed), *De Valera's Constitution and Ours: The Thomas Davis Lectures Series,* Dublin: Gill & Macmillan for RTE, 1988.

Grogan, Vincent, 'Towards the new Constitution' in MacManus, Francis (ed), *The Years of the Great Test,* Cork: The Mercier Press for RTE 1967, 161-72.

Kelly, J.M., *The Irish Constitution,* 3rd ed., Dublin: Butterworths 1994.

Kelsen, Hans, *General Theory of Law and State* [trans. Anders Wedberg], Cambridge, Mass.: Harvard University Press 1946.

Kelsen, Hans, *Pure Theory of Law* [trans. M. Knight], Berkeley, Cal.: University of California Press 1967.

Lee, J.J. (ed), *Ireland 1945-70,* Dublin: Gill & Macmillan 1979.

Litton, Frank (ed), *The Constitution of Ireland 1937-87,* Dublin: I.P.A. 1988.

Morgan, David Gwynn, *Constitutional Law of Ireland; The Law of the Executive, Legislature and Judicature,* 2nd ed., Dublin: The Round Hall Press 1990.

Prager, Jeffrey, *Building Democracy in Ireland,* Cambridge: Cambridge University Press 1986.

Wheare, K.C., *Modern Constitutions,* 2nd ed., Oxford: Oxford University Press 1966.

PERIODICALS

Akenson, D.H. and Fallin, J.F., 'The Irish Civil War and the Drafting of the Free State Constitution', *Éire-Ireland* Vol.5 (Nos. 1, 2, and 4, 1970).

Farrell, B., 'The Drafting of the Irish Free State Constitution', *The Irish Jurist* Vol. IV (New Series) (1969), 127–38.

O'Hanlon, Roderick J., 'A Constitution for a Free People', *Administration* Vol.15 (1967), 85–101.

Thompson, Brian, 'Living with a Supreme Court in Ireland', *Parliamentary Affairs* Vol. 44 No.1 (1991), 39–49.

GOVERNMENT PUBLICATIONS

Bunreacht na hÉireann, Dublin: Stationery Office.

Constitution of the Irish Free State, Dublin: Stationery Office.

Official Reports, Debates in the Houses of the Oireachtas (Dáil Éireann and Seanad Éireann), Dublin: Stationery Office.

Report of the Committee on the Constitution (1967), Dublin: Stationery Office.

Index